Pure

{ s e x }

ED YOUNG

Multnomah Books•Sisters, Oregon

PURE SEX
published by Multnomah Publishers, Inc.

© 1997 by Ed Young

International Standard Book Number: 1-57673-200-2

Printed in the United States of America

Most Scripture quotations are from:
New American Standard Bible (NASB)
© 1960, 1977 by the Lockman Foundation

Also quoted:
The Holy Bible, New International Version (NIV)
© 1973, 1984 by International Bible Society,
used by permission of Zondervan Publishing House

The King James Version (KJV)

The Living Bible (TLB)
© 1971 by Tyndale House Publishers

The Message, © 1993 by Eugene H. Peterson

Contemporary English Version copyright © 1995 American Bible Society

For information:
MULTNOMAH PUBLISHERS, INC.
POST OFFICE BOX 1720
SISTERS, OREGON 97759

97 98 99 00 01 02 03 04 — 10 9 8 7 6 5 4 3 2 1

Table of Contents

For my grandchildren, Lee Beth, E. J., Laurie, Landra, and Nicole. May they—and their generation—know the blessing of *pure sex*.

Acknowledgments

For thirteen weeks I had the privilege of presenting the material contained in this book to a weekly audience of approximately ten thousand adults. They sat and listened as I talked about "Sex in America." From that study, the book *Pure Sex* was born.

I am chiefly an oral communicator. Writing is a tedious task for me; speaking is my preferred medium. My research assistant, Leigh McLeroy, was an integral part of this project from the very beginning. Her research, reading, and gathering of facts, figures, and illustrations was invaluable to this series. When the "talking" was done, Leigh set about the task of "translating" my spoken words into written form, adding many timely and useful insights along the way. This project would have been delayed, if not impossible, without her diligence.

Also, let me thank Danny Aiken, Vice President of Academic Administration and Dean of the School of Theology at Southern Baptist Theological Seminary. Danny patiently reviewed the manuscript and encouraged me to persevere on more than one occasion when I was discouraged enough to consider abandoning the project altogether. His contribution to the chapter titled "Pure Lovemaking" was significant, while Danny's practical scholarship provided a solid sounding board.

Dorothy Patterson of Southeastern Baptist Theological Seminary was willing to read the manuscript as well. Her keen eye and sharp red pencil clarified much that was obscure or impractical. Dorothy added valuable insight as a theologian, wife, mother, and full-time student of life. Jane Hursey, Superintendent of Second Baptist School of Houston, Texas, read with a heart for young people and lent helpful insight into issues related to teenage sexuality. Diane Williams not only listened to the original study, but applied her love

7

of language to these pages, helping to make them more readable. Beverly Gambrell, my administrative assistant, not only covered countless office details which gave me time to concentrate on this book, but also read the manuscript on several occasions and offered practical suggestions throughout.

In this, as in every other endeavor, I am indebted to my wonderful family. My son Ed, pastor of the Fellowship of Las Colinas in Dallas, was the first to say, "Dad, you need to do a book on this subject." He encouraged me to listen to a series of messages by Bill Hybels, pastor of Willow Creek Community Church in suburban Chicago. The vivid and straightforward manner in which this gifted pastor dealt with sexuality before his congregation challenged me to proceed further in examining this sensitive area of life.

My son Ben, a pastor to single adults at Second Baptist Church of Houston, brought into focus the sexual pressures and temptations singles constantly face. Ben's awareness led him to say from the beginning, "Dad, you've got to write this down. You've got to put this in a book!"

My youngest son, Cliff, a member of the contemporary Christian group Caedmon's Call meets thousands of college students and "twenty-something" adults on the road each year, and he saw the need as well, adding with a hint of caution, "Dad, I hope you know you're swimming in barracuda-infested waters here." (He was right.)

Finally, my wife, Jo Beth, has been my "lab partner" in every aspect of life for almost forty years. While our sons were saying, "Dad, go for it!" Joby continually asked, "Edwin, are you *sure* you want to write this book?" No one knows better than she does what it means to love an imperfect person, body and soul. She is my lover, my partner, and the best friend I will ever know.

To all of these and to the many others I have not mentioned specifically by name, I am truly grateful. My prayer is that the end result may be used by God to teach us more about Himself and His excellent gifts, and ultimately, through our understanding and obedience, to bring glory to Himself.

ED YOUNG
HOUSTON, TEXAS

Introduction
Purity Makes a Comeback

The word *pure* is making a comeback...and it's about time. Like many words that go out of fashion and then reappear, *pure* is being used again with a slightly different meaning— and I believe, a better one.

While *pure* once described a person of almost saintly character, it is now most often used to describe not people, but things. "That is so *pure*," a young person might say today with a hint of admiration, even awe. What does it mean? If something is pure, what is it? At the very least, it's strong, undiluted, and inarguably fine. It's powerful and worthy of respect.

The title of this book, *Pure Sex*, is no oxymoron. It describes sex as its Designer intended it to be: worthy of awe, altogether right, undiminished by misuse, and untarnished by sin and selfishness. There is nothing lurid or cheap about our inherent sexuality. There never was. If there seems to be, it is only because modern man does not know what real sex is. He cannot, because he has separated the *creation* from its *Creator*, resulting in a hopelessly distorted view.

"That's ridiculous!" someone might say. "Of course we know what sex is all about. We are sexually liberated. We are informed viewers of Montel, Geraldo, and Sally. We've taken classes, read

9

books, seen movies. And many of us have experimented quite a bit. How can we be ignorant of sex when we live in a sex-saturated society?"

We can be ignorant because exposure does not equal knowledge, any more than frequent experimentation equals satisfaction. The fact that we are well-acquainted with sex does not mean that we understand it. Philosopher Peter Kreeft writes, "We do not think too much about sex, we think hardly at all about sex. Dreaming, fantasizing, feeling, experimenting—yes. But honest, look-it-in-the-face thinking? Hardly ever."[1]

We have an appetite for the mysteries of sex like no other people who ever lived, yet there is not a subject on the planet about which we have more information and less insight. Book after book and study after study continue to analyze sex exhaustively. But the fact that we have so many books does not mean that we are experts. It means we are still looking for answers.

So why yet another book on sex? Because while we may be stuffed with "how to" sexual information, we're still starved for wholeness; we still seek satisfaction. And since all truth is God's truth, we desperately need to hear from Him about sex. Former United States Surgeon General Jocelyn Elders said, "We've taught our children what to do in the front seat of the car, now we need to teach them what to do in the back seat." Let me suggest that when one out of five teenage girls has been pregnant by the time she is nineteen, the mechanics of the back seat are no mystery. But pure sex is.

When (depending on what survey you read) one-fourth to one-half of married men and women have been unfaithful to their mates; when one of every six Americans carries a sexually transmitted disease; when AIDS is the leading cause of death for twenty-six- to forty-four-year-olds; and yet lack of desire is a common complaint heard by sex therapists and counselors, more information on sex is not the solution. We don't need more pamphlets and programs and politically correct slogans like "No glove, no love." We need to be introduced to a new (or actually a very old) way of looking at things. We need to rediscover pure sex.

The pure sex we need to rediscover is not simply a matter of mechanics. Sex is not only something we *do*. It is something we *are*. Sex is a part of our identity as men and women created in the image of God, and it is a beautiful symbol of our relationship with Him. Human sexuality simply cannot be understood apart from relationship. The sex that men's clubs and pornographers peddle is a gross distortion, light years removed from the real thing. Richard Foster, writing in *Money, Sex, and Power*, says of those who misuse and exploit sex, "They totally eliminate relationships and restrain sexuality to the narrow confines of the genitals. They have made sex trivial."[2]

Foster is absolutely on target! As a result of our trivializing sex, an amazing thing has occurred. We have become a culture that is more and more sexually active, but less and less sexually satisfied. We have unprecedented sexual freedom coupled with unprecedented sexual disappointment. We are caught in a deceptive trap of our own design. Far too many of us are physically sick, psychologically scarred, emotionally unsatisfied, and spiritually numb. We've abandoned the real "joy of sex" for the pursuit of the next sexual fix, and we have come to believe that passion is something that lasts five minutes on a good day! We've accepted an imitation for the genuine article—and are only just beginning to realize the tragedy of our error.

We still feel hunger, but more and more of us are choosing to pass up the steak for its sizzle. Our sexual appetite has gone awry— something C. S. Lewis observed nearly four decades ago: "Suppose you came to a country where you could fill a theater simply by bringing a covered plate to the stage and slowly lifting the cover so as to let everyone see, just before the lights went out, that it contained a mutton chop or a bit of bacon, would you not think that in that country something had gone wrong with the appetite for food? And would not anyone who had grown up in a different world think there was something equally queer about the state of the sex instinct among us?"[3] We are a culture preoccupied, tantalized, and fascinated by all manner of things sexual, often more interested in teasing our strange desires than in satisfying our natural ones.

We live in a broken-down world that one author suggests invites two sexual extremes: avoidance or worship. "[Avoidance] has to do with fear; [worship] lust. In *The End of Sex,* George Leonard maintains that sexuality, with its powder kegs of guilt and disillusionment, is simply not worth the trouble. Add on top of that the fear of disease, a broken heart, and a failed marriage or two, and sex simply makes people too vulnerable. The other extreme is excess. The attitude toward sex today is often one of worship. The thirst for intimacy and transcendence, lacking better options, gets routed into the closest thing many can find to a miracle: sex."[4]

How then do we avoid the trap of sexual extremes? How do we develop a desire for pure sex? For many the journey will begin with a growing dissatisfaction in the myriad hollow sexual imitations:

- when a one-night stand provides more grief than relief
- when an affair is discovered and a marriage shattered
- when yet another dream of real intimacy yields only a few meaningless acts of intercourse
- when a heart or a home is broken
- when a relationship that once seemed exciting quickly becomes dull and routine
- when a devastating diagnosis calls a lifestyle into question
- or when "Is that all there is?" is asked…over and over again

Where can we turn when our sexual lives yield nothing but despair and disappointment? Let me suggest a radical plan. We can turn to the eternal source of all wisdom: God. And why not? He understands the sexual desires of men and women because He is their Creator. That means He's the Creator of sex. He is not silent on sexual matters. His Word addresses the unique sexual challenges proposed by both singleness and marriage. It also addresses the timeless issues of temptation, desire, and fulfillment.

What do we have to lose? All that the current experts have managed to give us in terms of sexual enlightenment has not satisfied our longing for something transcendent, something pure and beautiful. Instead, we've settled for what some have called "nutra-sex"—

artificial substitutes for pure sex that eventually cause cancer—both in relationships and in the soul. I believe it is time to trade "nutra-sex" for pure sex. Through God (and only through Him) we can gain an understanding of sex as a glorious gift, meant by its Creator to be fully expressed and enjoyed in covenant relationship.

This is a book for every man or woman who has struggled in the area of their sexuality and wondered how to make what is wrong, right. It is primarily for those whose lives have been marred by their sexual choices—in other words, for those who have messed up. But it is also for those who have managed so far to choose wisely—that is, for adults who are leading upright sexual lives. Finally, it is for those who are just beginning to make decisions about their God-given sexuality—for teenagers. It offers what I believe is the best plan for sexual sanity and real sexual satisfaction anywhere, namely, God's plan.

Because *His* way works, I challenge you to try it. I think you will see that anything *but* His plan leads at best to second-rate sexuality. Jesus Christ said, "You shall know the truth, and the truth shall make you free" (John 8:32). Let me invite you to join others in discovering God's liberating, freeing truth about our sexuality. I can't promise that the road to pure sex will be easy—but I can promise that the adventure will be exhilarating and the results life changing. By putting His principles into practice, we can experience the thrill of pure sex...and maybe, just maybe, rediscover true passion in a love-starved world.

PART ONE

Pursuing God's Best

CHAPTER ONE

Sex

An American Obsession

Make no mistake. Ours is a sex-saturated culture. You might even say that sex has become an American obsession. From magazines and billboards to the Internet and the entertainment industry, we are bombarded with sexual messages and sexual innuendos. *Sex* is the most frequently used search word on the information superhighway. It is often the hook used to attract viewers to mainline talk shows and films. In fact, one of the highest-rated television shows of recent years was a *Seinfeld* episode that dealt openly with the once-taboo subject of masturbation. That single episode, entitled "The Wager," spawned its own web site, where net-surfers could comment on its content and discuss their own views on masturbation, along with those of *Seinfeld* characters Jerry, Elaine, Kramer, and George!

And sex is not just for entertainment. From royalty in England to politicians in Washington, from pastors in pulpits to business executives in corner offices, our culture is marked by an unusual, overwhelming interest in anything sexual. Sex is used to sell everything from perfume to high performance vehicles, to amuse, to titillate, and even to make political statements. It is *the* main ingredient in modern entertainment programming, with MTV and the major movie studios serving up a steady diet of sex in every conceivable form.

Based on what is depicted by the media, any alien visitor to America would likely conclude that every person over the age of twelve is sexually active, that marriage is the *last* place to look for sexual satisfaction, that faithfulness is a nostalgic dream, and that even the sickest of sexual perversions is nothing less than every citizen's "inalienable right."

THE SILENT CHURCH

This would be true, of course, unless they happened to visit the church. Then they would probably wonder whatever became of sex. They might never hear it mentioned at all—or perhaps only spoken of in whispers, or condemning tones. Historically, to its shame, the church has either ignored the God-given gift of human sexuality or smothered it with an avalanche of "Thou shalt not's."

Even St. Augustine (A.D. 354–430), whose *Confessions* has inspired millions, concluded that since sex has caused mankind such struggle and heartbreak, he wished God had dreamed up a better idea! Augustine no doubt wrote out of his own personal misfortune with sex, which produced an illegitimate child and brought his heart great disillusionment.

While Augustine missed the mark by a mile with his negative conclusion, he was right about one thing: *Sex was God's idea.* As the designer of this wonderful, mysterious, and powerful gift, God knows what it can and cannot do and how it should and should not be expressed. And the sexuality He created was pure sex—sex that is right and good, meant to be fully enjoyed in its intended framework. That's right! God made pure sex, and He is purely pleased with it as a valuable part of His creation. Any pain or conflict His gift may cause is not the result of faulty design but of our own misuse and misunderstanding.

If modern culture has oversold sex and the contemporary church has ignored it, where can the truth about our God-given sexuality be found? Thankfully, there *is* a source that has never been silent or wrong about sex and contains (along with the ugly and the tragic) everything that is true and lovely and right about it. That source is the Bible. It is an ancient book that combines the mystery of the ages with the practicality of a modern bestseller. A book that is both God-breathed and astonishingly earthy, gritty and real (2 Timothy 3:16–17).

The Bible never shies away from speaking of sex. It tells it like it is, from the rapture of married lovemaking to the agony of adultery, and from the struggle for sexual purity to the ever-present temptations of desire. Its pages are populated with real people and their real passions. Its intrigue would put an award-winning miniseries to shame and its seductive language of love would make a straight-laced librarian blush. (Try the Song of Solomon in a modern translation if you think I'm exaggerating!)

Does the Bible have anything meaningful to say to those who have experienced plenty of sex—but have yet to discover the ecstasy of pure sex? It does indeed. Does it deal straight up with the desires of those who are single? You bet it does. Does it make married love sound exciting? Absolutely! Well, then, how about the darker side of human sexuality? Do people in this book understand what it's like to deal with sexual addiction? A one-night stand? Lust? As a matter of fact, they do. But above all, the Bible places sex in its proper framework—and that is a total, intimate, lifetime commitment of marriage.

Even John Gray, the author of the popular *Men Are from Mars, Women Are from Venus,* concludes that sex and commitment are definitely made for each other. "What makes sex really great is love. The more you get to know someone and continue to grow in intimacy and love, the more the sexual experience has a chance to thrive."[1] Dr. Gray is not a biblical scholar, but he has echoed the heart of a biblical truth: Sex thrives in an atmosphere of committed love. God's design for pure sex reserves its full expression for the marriage relationship: one man, with one woman, for life.

Some would rush to label His design "stifling"—but perhaps the time has come to reexamine that view. Consider these words that appeared (oddly enough) in the *Wall Street Journal:* "The United States has a drug problem and a high school sex problem and welfare problem and an AIDS problem and a rape problem. None of this will go away until more people in positions of responsibility are willing to come forward and explain, in frankly moral terms, that some of the things people do nowadays are wrong."[2] The article went on to suggest that we bring the word *sin* out of hiding and begin to use it again without laughing or winking at one another.

Maybe, just maybe, we're beginning to suspect that we have been sold a cheap bill of goods where sex is concerned. Maybe we're beginning to wonder whether the so-called sexual revolution was a tidal wave of freedom as advertised, or a trap door which has led to untold disaster. Maybe the sexual icons of our culture, from Alfred Kinsey, Masters and Johnson, and Hugh Hefner, to Sheri Hite, Madonna, and Dr. Ruth, *don't* have all the answers. Maybe there is more to sexual satisfaction after all than unbridled lust, grimly perfected technique, and the avoidance of deadly disease.

BEYOND THE HYPE

When a team of researchers at the University of Chicago released a long-awaited scientific study titled "Sex in America," the results were surprising, primarily in their tameness. While the Kinsey studies of the late 1940s caused something of a national scandal, the Chicago study barely raised a collective eyebrow. What it revealed was that the majority of Americans claim to be monogamous, that married couples report having more frequent sex than their single counterparts, and that homosexuality is not as prevalent in our society as we have been led to believe.

Other data collected indicated that couples who consider themselves religious or claim a church affiliation are just as "sexual" as those who do not, and that the married women reporting the highest degree of sexual satisfaction were conservative Protestants! Additionally, over half of all respondents agreed that their religious beliefs *had* guided their sexual behavior.

These results hint that we are moving away from the tendency to separate sex from the whole of life—and that is good news! Far from being an isolated act with the significance of a sneeze, sex is one of the most intimate, life-altering, profound, and deeply spiritual experiences available to man. It is the most natural high our bodies can experience. Sex is a strong, strong force, and what we choose to do with it affects not only our own lives, but other lives as well. In fact, our collective view of sex can predict the fate of our very society.

Scholar J. D. Unwin wrote years ago in *Sex and Culture,* "In human records there is no instance of a society retaining its energy after a complete new generation has inherited a tradition which does not insist on prenuptial and postnuptial continence."[3] In other words, societies that place no value on premarital chastity and marital fidelity simply do not thrive. Unwin studied hundreds of years of history and concluded that the health and longevity of nations directly corresponded to the value placed on sexual purity. Societies whose sexual mores were strong prevailed. Those whose sexual mores were weak no longer exist. Could this be what ancient Israel's King Solomon meant when he spoke of the "total ruin" which awaited those who disregarded God's commands in this area (Proverbs 5:14)?

Imagine! Ancient history and modern surveys confirm what God has always said: that sex is a multifaceted gift of deep importance, and that chastity or lifelong marriage is the safest, surest, and richest setting for its expression. That's pure sex—and it is no contradiction in terms. Pure, undefiled, undiluted sex is what God intended for us from the very beginning. If we make "safe sex" our highest aim, we will fall far short of the awesome sexual experience God has in mind for us as His children. He desires much more than that for you and me.

WHY GOD MADE SEX

God created sex for two reasons. One is obvious. One is not. First the obvious: God gave us sex for the purpose of procreation (Genesis 1:27–28). Sexual intercourse is the means by which we conceive children and populate our families and the world. It is a creative, life-giving act. God could have chosen any number of ways for the human race to multiply, but in His wisdom, He gave us sexual bodies that fit together perfectly, a natural desire for the opposite sex, and the ability to create new life through that physical union.

But God also made sex for the purpose of pleasure (Song of Solomon 7:6–13). The pleasure of sex was an intentional part of His divine design, not a serendipitous by-product. He *meant* for sex to be a powerfully pleasurable experience. God could have made sex merely functional—but He did not. Instead, He made it to be a thrilling, passionate act—full of potential for physical delight.

This is the one sexual truth that the Church has hedged throughout history. Augustine wrongly concluded that sex should be for procreation, nothing more. Aquinas (1225–1274) held that a sex act that included the possibility of conception (even rape) was better than one that did not afford that possibility. And Martin Luther (1483–1546) wrote in *The Estate of Marriage,* "Intercourse is never without sin; but God excuses it by His grace because the estate of marriage is His work, and He preserves in and through the sin all that good which He has implanted and blessed in marriage."

But the Bible begs to differ. God's Word speaks openly of the pleasures of sex, as in this exchange between King Solomon and his bride, the Shulamite: "Awake, O north wind, and come, wind of the south; make my garden breathe out fragrance, let its spices be wafted abroad. May my beloved come into his garden and eat its choice fruits!" Then, "I have come into my garden, my sister, my bride; I have gathered my myrrh along with my balsam. I have eaten my honeycomb and my honey; I have drunk my wine and my milk. Eat, friends; drink and imbibe deeply, O lovers" (Song of Solomon 4:16–5:1).

Does this passage even begin to hint that ravenous, expressive sex in marriage is a sin? Does it describe a grim, joyless couple whose sexuality is distasteful to them and to their God? Not on your life! It sounds instead like a husband and wife who enjoy to the fullest the pleasures of their God-designed sexuality, a couple who are free and unashamed in their desire for one another.

Historically, we've either made too little of sex—or too much. The ancients viewed sex as a dangerous evil; modern man has made it an idol. In truth, it is neither. Somewhere between the extremes of the Protestant Reformation (the 1500s) and the sexual revolution (the 1960s) lies the truth about pure sex. It is a part of the total fabric of life, yet it is different. It is a powerful force, perhaps the most powerful on earth, and one that requires constraint to be safely and fully enjoyed. Jagged lightning and a power plant both generate electricity—but most folks who know something about voltage would rather get theirs from the plant!

To those who would argue that we should treat sex like any other human impulse (and many today do argue just that), C. S. Lewis poignantly answers: "All the others [impulses], we admit, have to be bridled. Absolute obedience to your instinct for self-preservation is what we call cowardice; to your acquisitive impulse, avarice. Even sleep must be resisted if you're a sentry. But every unkindness and breach of faith seems to be condoned provided that the object aimed at is 'four bare legs in a bed.' It is like having a morality in which stealing fruit is considered wrong—unless you steal nectarines."[4]

This powerful thing that God created is not simple. It is a complex and wonderful gift that we cannot easily conform to our own requirements. We can't have it both ways—at least not very well. We can't worship sex and at the same time treat it casually. We can't deny the bounds of morality and hope to preserve our integrity. We can't pursue unrestrained sexual freedom and hope to avoid the unconscious crafting of our own chains. Our confusion can only be resolved if we look for the truth about sex from the source of *all* truth. Only then can we begin to make some sense out of the immense mystery of our sexuality.

A MYSTERIOUS, SENSITIVE SUBJECT

Even though we are exposed to sexual images every day of our lives, sex is still surrounded by a certain mystique and a great deal of angst. Sex has the power to thrill, intimidate, delight, anger, excite, frighten, calm, or confuse. Whether it evokes a sense of guilt or a sense of pleasure, sex seldom fails to generate at least a passing interest. Even children come to understand that there is something special, something different, about their sexuality. An event as innocent as bath time can become the catalyst for sexual curiosity, as the following anecdote illustrates.

A mother was giving her three-year-old son a bath. As she washed him, he began a playful game, pointing to himself and asking, "What's this?"

He pointed to his eye. "Mom! What's this?"

"That's your eye, sweetie."

He tugged at his ear. "What's this?"

"That's your ear."

Then his mouth. "Mom! What's this?"

"That's your mouth, silly."

Then she continued naming his body parts as he traveled down. "That's your chest. Ummm…that's your belly button."

Then, predictably, her son pointed a little lower, and before he could ask, "What's this?" his poor mom had passed out cold on the bathroom tile.[5] Now, she should have seen that he was headed south, anatomically speaking, but somehow we parents are never quite prepared for those "teachable moments" when they arrive. Instinctively, or by our reactions, our children come to understand that there is a mystique about sexual things, that they are somehow different.

So let's be honest and say up front that sex is a sensitive subject. I believe every individual would agree that when we begin to seriously examine our sexuality, we are dealing with a very, very sensitive area of life. Many people hide painful sexual scars from the past and carry their accompanying emotional baggage in a way that makes true intimacy for them an all-but-impossible dream. Far too many men and women live a continuing nightmare because of a sexual incident (or incidents) that occurred in their childhood or teenage years. Still others struggle with sexual guilt—either real or self-imposed. Some deal daily with sexual addictions, lust, affairs, pornography, or homosexuality.

What is it that makes problems in the sexual area so painful? Why do so many of these wounds never seem to heal? Why have God's liberating forgiveness and healing eluded so many? Why is sex—and our handling of it—such a delicate subject?

Sex is sensitive because it is inherently, undeniably *personal*. It involves our body and our soul. It is not something that is far removed from us. We are not, and can never be, comfortably distanced from it. Writing to his friends in the ancient city of Corinth, the apostle Paul warned, "Some of you say, 'We can do anything we want to.' But I tell you that not everything is good for us. So I refuse to let anything have power over me. Don't be immoral in matters of sex. That is a sin against your own body in a way that no other sin is" (1 Corinthians 6:12, 18, CEV).

There is, of course, no hierarchy of sin. There is no sin that is more "acceptable" to God than another, because *no sin at all is acceptable to Him.* But, because sexual sin is a sin not only against God, but against our very own bodies, its consequences are devastating to us in a way that those of other sins may not be.

Think about it. When Hitler was systematically attacking the continent of Europe during World War II, Allied forces joined in a united defense. American soldiers fought and died on foreign soil, and the conflict certainly took its toll on our country—but we sustained nowhere near the damage that Britain or Austria or Poland suffered. Why? Because the war was not fought on our own soil.

By contrast, battles over sexual sin are always fought at home. They take place "on our own soil," on and within our physical bodies. There is no escaping the shrapnel of sexual sin. Sex outside of God's established parameters impoverishes a man or a woman the way a war at home impoverishes a nation. It's a little like robbing a bank. I'm sure there is a certain "high" in pulling off a successful crime, like a bank robbery. (As I recall, Butch Cassidy and the Sundance Kid made it look like a whole lot of fun for a while.) But what happens to bank robbers with few exceptions? They get caught. And when they do, they lose everything. Their lives are indelibly marked by their crime.

That's what sexual sin is like. It doesn't make you a richer person in the end. It makes you poorer. And if you are the least bit sensitive to God, especially if you are a Christian, you will experience a heaviness of spirit that you simply cannot shake. You will be affected—physically, mentally, emotionally, and spiritually, because sex is a *personal* thing. You can't get away from it. It is within you and within me.

THE TRUTH ABOUT GUILT

In spite of our society's liberated views, sex and guilt are frequent partners these days. In fact, the two are virtually inseparable in the lives of many. Why is that? And how can we know with any certainty whether the guilt that we may associate with sex is true guilt or false guilt?

I believe we experience guilt for two very good reasons. First, many of us feel guilty about sex because there is sexual sin in our lives. It's that simple. We have "broken the law" sexually, and our conscience confirms what we already know: we have done wrong. "Your sin will find you out," Moses told the people of Israel (Numbers 32:23), and inevitably, ours will too.

Second, many of us feel guilty with regard to sex because we are not sure what is right and what is wrong. I've received many sincere letters from married couples who want to do right sexually but are afraid that their particular desires or practices are not acceptable to God. So they carry a vague but persistent sense of guilt about their sexual lives that may not be justified. "Should I feel guilty for having a sexual thought?" some ask, or "Is my particular desire wrong?" "Should I ask forgiveness when I experience sexual temptation?" others want to know, or "Was it my fault I was molested as a child?"

If I could sit down with each one of these hurting individuals and reassure them, I would. I would tell them that each of us— young, old, male, female—is created a sexual being by God Himself. We quite naturally have sexual thoughts and emotions. To feel ashamed about our God-given sexuality is wrong. To take responsibility for the sins of others is wrong. That is false guilt. And to *continue* to live in shame or guilt over a past sexual sin that has been confessed to God and repented of is just as wrong. In essence, it is calling God a liar when He says, as He does in 1 John 1:9, "If we confess our sins, He is faithful and righteous to forgive us our sins and to cleanse us from all unrighteousness."

How do we know if the guilt we are experiencing is true guilt or false guilt? We must measure it by a standard that is truer than our own heart: the Word of God. There *are* a handful of things God specifically says no to in the sexual area. To know what these things are, and to avoid them, gives us the confidence that we are sexually clean before God.

First, God says no to sexual intercourse outside of marriage. We'll talk more about why this is so later, but for now, just know that extramarital and premarital sex (either adultery or fornication) are forbidden by God (see 1 Corinthians 6:18; 7:2–5; Hebrews 13:4).

Second, God says no to sex with a member of our immediate family. That is incest, and God specifically forbids it (see Leviticus 18:6–18).

Third, God says no to sex between persons of the same gender. He repeatedly warns against this practice, known as homosexuality (see Romans 1:26–27; 1 Corinthians 6:9).

Fourth, God says no to sex with animals, or bestiality (see Exodus 22:19; Leviticus 20:13–16).

Fifth, God says no to indulging in sexual fantasy for anyone other than your marriage partner. That is lust (see Matthew 5:27–28).

Finally, God says no to sex that is painful, forced, or violent. This is abuse, and it is not a part of His design (see 1 Corinthians 13:4–7; Philippians 2:3–4).

These six things which God forbids are not my personal opinion. They are His word. They would not necessarily be viewed wrong by the majority in a national poll. They do not mirror current psychological theories, sociological trends, or cultural mores. Our culture actually embraces some of these practices and chooses to overlook or tolerate the others. But to live outside of these divine laws is to make camp in a war zone. It is dangerous, perhaps even deadly.

Persist in breaking any one of these laws, and you will experience payday someday—in your body, your psyche, your lifestyle, or all three. It will happen. It always does. Man has looked for sexual loopholes for generations and has yet to discover a single one. Guilt that stems from the breaking of these divine laws is true guilt. It is as simple as that.

It would be easier if God gave us a more detailed list of practices that are forbidden, but He did not. His Word reads more like a love story than a how-not-to manual, a fact for which I am deeply grateful. The above list does not cover every sexual possibility and no list could be exhaustive. There is a wide world of sexual expression available to every husband and wife. How can they know what practices are right for their marriage? The following questions are designed to help them discern for themselves what should or should not be a part of their lovemaking:

- Does this particular activity increase our oneness and intimacy?

- Is this activity agreed-upon and mutually pleasing?

- Is this a practice we would like for our children to engage in one day when they marry?

- Can we enjoy this with a clear conscience before God?

- Is this practice safe, medically, emotionally, and physically?

If a husband and wife can answer yes to these questions in the gray areas of sexual expression, they can feel confident that their actions are acceptable and right—both in the sight of God and in the context of their unique marital relationship.

FOUR THINGS THAT EVERYONE SHOULD KNOW

There are four basic truths about sex that everyone—male or female, married or single, young or old—should know.

First, _sex was God's idea._ (See Genesis 2). Hugh Hefner didn't invent sex. Madonna has introduced nothing original. Masters and Johnson didn't happen on the sexual differences between men and women in the last half of the twentieth century. God established sex. He brought it into being. It is His gift to us. It is part of His creation, and its design bears the very signature of the divine. Look at it: "Then the LORD God said, 'It is not good for the man to be alone; I will make him a helper suitable for him'" (Genesis 2:18).

Throughout the creation story, God calls His handiwork "good" and even "very good." But that man should be alone, God said, was "not good." He knew that His first created man, Adam, needed companionship in the form of another. He saw the need. "I will make..."

God said, and He took the initiative. In the beginning, God made two distinctly different, sexual beings. It was His idea.

The second important truth for us to understand is that *human sexuality is unique.* The Bible makes it clear that there is more involved in human sexuality than the satisfaction of an instinctual, physical urge: "And out of the ground the LORD God formed every beast of the field and every bird of the sky, and brought them to the man to see what he would call them; and whatever the man called a living creature, that was its name. And the man gave names to all the cattle, and to the birds of the sky, and to every beast of the field, but for Adam there was not found a helper suitable for him" (Genesis 2:19–20).

We are not merely animals! We are created in the image of God (Genesis 1:26–27), and our sexuality is more complex and multi-faceted than the urge of animals to mate. There was not one thing in the beautiful and diverse animal kingdom that satisfied Adam's deepest longing for companionship. He knew it and God knew it. Adam could not communicate with the animals. There was nothing in them that corresponded to his humanity, which bore the very image of God. Something different, something unique was required to complement him, hence God created woman.

The third great truth we need to remember is that *sex involves every aspect of our being.* Our culture would argue that sex is a basic and straightforward need, similar to the hunger for food or the instinct for self-preservation. But to describe it in those terms is to minimize its significance and grossly oversimplify its meaning. Sex is infinitely more than an animalistic urge. It is a total union between two who are different—male and female—but whose nature is similar. The first man and the first woman were designed to fit one another in a union that was more than physical. It was an emotional, relational, and spiritual bull's-eye.

Notice the sequence in the creation account. God created the animals, male and female together. Then He created man. Then He created man's counterpart: woman. What was she? She was the other half of man. He was the other half of her. Adam recognized this "whole being fit" not when he first had sex with Eve, but when he first laid eyes on her! "This is now bone of my bones, and flesh of my flesh," he said. "She shall be called Woman, because she was taken out of Man" (Genesis 2:23).

He knew that she was *it*. It was as if Adam had said, "Eureka! I've found it! Here's the rest of me!" His body, his soul, his spirit recognized her "rightness" for him, and he knew that she offered what the animals he had named could not. Sex involves the whole being—the physical, the psychological, the emotional, and the spiritual. In God's perfect design, these components are not to be separated. To do so is to go against the very grain of the created universe.

Finally, we need to understand that *sex requires boundaries*. We are not to share ourselves sexually with just anyone. Because sex involves the whole person and is not an unconnected physical act, its expression must be fiercely protected and held in honor. God's intent for Adam was a complete, free, shameless, and beautiful sexual relationship with one woman (Eve) for life. His plan for His very Son, Jesus Christ, was a committed, vital, and passionate life of chastity as an unmarried person.

His plan is the same today: fidelity for those who are married, chastity for those who are single. Not denial of our inherent sexuality, but diversity in its expression. A married man or woman is no more sexual in nature than a single man or woman—but the expression of that sexuality through the act of sexual intercourse is reserved for marriage: "For this cause a man shall leave his father and his mother, and shall cleave to his wife; and they shall become one flesh. And the man and his wife were both naked and were not ashamed" (Genesis 2:24–25).

This word, spoken by both Jesus and the apostle Paul in the New Testament, is more than just a commentary on two people named Adam and Eve. (After all, they had no parents to leave!) Instead, it is the birth record of an ongoing, holy, human institution called marriage. It describes an exclusive relationship entered into by two where, "naked and unashamed," they become one with each other. Sex is the result of their intimate commitment—not the other way around.

Marriage is the home God designed for physical sexual expression between man and woman. He established boundaries around their sexual intimacy not to be a killjoy, but to ensure maximum joy! He meant for sex to be a blessing, not a burden; to be a delight and not a disaster. G. K. Chesterton once said he understood the chief aim of Christianity's rule and order was "to give good things a chance to run wild."[6]

Think of sex as yet another good thing created by God, whose established parameters encourage freedom, not bondage. In marriage, there is the freedom for a man and wife to fully know one another through God's beautiful gift of sexual intercourse. Their union is exclusive—and is expressed emotionally, mentally, spiritually, and physically.

In singleness, there is the freedom to invest deeply in a greater number of emotionally, mentally, or spiritually intimate relationships. But singles are to treasure and honor physical sexuality through celibacy, realizing that the full "knowing" that comes with intercourse is a gift too fine to squander on anything less than a total commitment to one person for life.

Only those who honor God's boundaries for sex will know the joy of true sexual freedom. Men and women who disregard those boundaries will learn inevitable and painful lessons in bondage, not in freedom. *His* way works. That promise alone should be reason enough to trust Him and to discover for ourselves the joy inherent in pure sex.

CHAPTER TWO

The State
of the Union
Sexual Integrity in Marriage

I
n 1993 one of the most talked-about films was *Indecent Proposal*. It told of a young married couple overwhelmed with financial problems who was offered a way out of bankruptcy by a handsome, middle-aged multimillionaire. What was his indecent proposal? That the young wife spend one night alone with him—in return for a cool million.

Of course, not many struggling couples ever meet a tycoon offering a fortune for a single night of extramarital sex, but then, this scenario was conceived in Hollywood!

An indecent proposal. A million dollars for a one-night stand. Bizarre as it was, the idea intrigued a lot of folks. Everyone was talking about the film. "Hard as it may be to believe," one newspaper columnist wrote, "for one brief, boring moment, this utterly unbelievable movie had every talk show and columnist in America possessed by the notion of people having sex because they're broke—this in a country where people generally have sex because they're bored."[1]

Ordinary and famous people were asked, "Would you be unfaithful to your spouse for $1 million? For $10 million? For $100 million?" But no one asked what I believe are more revealing questions: "Would you be unfaithful to your mate for $5? For $10?" Why are they more revealing questions? Because if you would be unfaithful for a $100 million but not for $5, the issue is not whether you would consider infidelity, but at what price you would consent to cheat.

The film's proposal was probably termed "indecent" not because it involved adultery, but because it involved money. Peter Kreeft writes that our modern society "treat[s] sex like money—as a medium of exchange of mere fun and convenience, not a holy thing in itself" and treats money like sex: "not that the true sense of the sacred, the holy and the awesome is attached to it. But something quite close to that: it is worshipped, it is treated as an end."[2]

But the true indecency of such a proposal is that it cheapens a beautiful gift of God and undermines the institution meant to be its home: marriage. "Let marriage be held in honor among all," the writer of the Book of Hebrews urged, "and let the marriage bed be undefiled; for fornicators and adulterers God will judge" (Hebrews 13:4).

In other words, there is never room for a third party (or parties) in a marriage relationship—for any reason. As the foolhardy couple in Indecent Proposal soon discovered, sexual infidelity (even consensual infidelity) destroys the very foundation of marital trust and intimacy. The all-too-common disclaimer of the unfaithful, "It didn't mean anything," is insulting. (Just ask the adulterer's spouse what it meant to him or to her!) There is no such thing as a "meaningless affair"; regardless of the intent, the unfaithful participants will wind up spiritually and emotionally impoverished, their marriage dishonored, and their marriage bed defiled.

The words of God's inspired instruction regarding fidelity are not randomly chosen. They are specific and important. Marriage is to be honored because it is a sacred covenant. Whether a couple is married in a cathedral or a courthouse, they are making a covenant with one another and with God to honor their union. This "one man with one woman for life" commitment is the natural habitat created by God for human sexual expression. It is meant to be permanent and exclusive (see Matthew 19:6). It is to be "held in honor," meaning that our view of it should be exceedingly high.

God calls those who are having sex outside of the marriage covenant "fornicators and adulterers," two words not used much today. Fornication is simply intercourse between two unmarried persons; adultery refers to sexual intercourse between a married person and one who is not his or her mate. Both of these acts destroy the inherent purity of the marriage bed. They are not just indecent, they are morally wrong, and God says He will judge them.

Why is God so insistent that sexual intercourse take place exclusively in marriage? Because of the very nature of sex itself. Sexual intercourse is a soul-uniting act. The apostle Paul said, "Do you not know that he who unites himself with a prostitute is one with her in body?" (1 Corinthians 6:16, NIV). He based his remark on the teaching of Genesis 2 that "the two shall become one." In some mysterious, inexplicable way, sex joins two people permanently. It is unique. It has special significance.

Author and professor Lewis Smedes says the impact of intercourse "goes beyond the earth-shaking orgasm and even the conscious self-sharing of two personalities. It cannot be captured on the frame of a pornographic film or even in an erotic masterpiece. It cannot be tested with electrodes attached to the erogenous zones of the body. It can only, in the last analysis, be believed. Coitus is an act that typifies—and in a way not made rationally clear—seals a life-union between two people. Therefore, it is only proper for those who intend a life-union together. Marriage alone qualifies people for sexual intercourse."[3]

The traditional Protestant marriage vows reflect this intent, with both partners promising to "love, honor, comfort and keep" one another, "forsaking all others," as long as they both shall live. The old Anglican vows further allude to the undefiled nature of sex in marriage when bride and groom address one another with the words, "with my body I thee worship."

WHAT'S GONE WRONG?

We've seen that sex in marriage is meant to be exclusive—and yet affairs today are common. We live in a society where over half of all marriages end in divorce. The majority of those who do divorce point to infidelity as the chief reason for their breakup. All kinds of affairs exist today. There is the office affair (they were just caring co-workers). The good neighbor affair (they were just being friendly). The cup of coffee affair (they just wanted to talk). The sales meet-ing/convention affair (they were just lonely). Depending on what survey you consult, anywhere from one-fourth to two-thirds of all married men have been unfaithful and nearly as many women have strayed.

I have had the opportunity to conduct hundreds of weddings in the last thirty-five years, and I can tell you this: Most couples who marry do intend to be faithful. At the marriage altar, most, if not all, would decry the idea of becoming sexually intimate with someone other than their mate. The marital vows that promise exclusivity and honor are repeated with conviction and firm resolve, in part because the two people making them are helplessly and hopelessly in love. They cannot imagine desiring or pursuing an adulterous relation-ship.

So if marriage is meant to be exclusive, if sex is intended only for the mutual enjoyment of husband and wife, and if the idea of adul-tery is far from the minds of brides and grooms, then why do affairs take place? How does sexual infidelity happen? If we can under-stand the process that typically leads to adultery, I believe we can in turn safeguard our marriages, prevent the defilement of the marriage bed by an affair, and begin to practice the kind of positive fidelity that fortifies the true freedom, maturity, and growth of both spouses.

THE ANATOMY OF AN AFFAIR

If it happened today, in our time and culture, the headlines would read something like this: "AFFAIR OF ISRAELI KING RESULTS IN ILLEGITIMATE HEIR, MURDER!" Following would be a lurid description of the rooftop bath that set things in motion and per-haps a firsthand account of David and Bathsheba's liaison, given by the servant who pressed her ear to the wall of the king's bedchamber on that fateful day. Unnamed hospital sources would report the baby's birth (if it was allowed to be born at all), and secret military sources would describe doomed Uriah's last moments on the battlefield. Then the media would naturally report on its own coverage of the entire story. We would know exactly *how* these events took place; we would not know *why*.

The real story behind King David's "dangerous liaison" with Bathsheba is even more significant than the details of the act itself. Writer Walter Wangerin Jr. says, "Adultery is never a sudden, spontaneous, totally unexpected act. It is always preceded by a longer drama, at the beginning of which *you are not helpless.*"[4]

David's affair began long before it culminated in his well-documented one-night stand. All affairs do. Let's dissect one of history's most famous indiscretions and examine the structure—the anatomy—of an affair.

1. A Seemingly Inconsequential Rift

Every relationship is full of moments of great consequence that, at the time, seem inconsequential. King David and his young wife experienced such a moment prior to David's affair with Bathsheba. David had triumphantly returned the Ark of the Covenant (the visible symbol of God's presence with His people, Israel) to its rightful place in Jerusalem. It had languished for years in a foreign land among foreign people, and David brought it home.

> And David went and brought up the ark of God from the house of Obed-edom into the city of David with gladness. And so it was, that when the bearers of the ark of the LORD had gone six paces, he sacrificed an ox and a fatling. And David was dancing before the LORD with all his might, and David was wearing a linen ephod. So David and all the house of Israel were bringing up the ark of the LORD with shouting and the sound of the trumpet. (2 Samuel 6:12b–15)

Make that *almost* all of the house of Israel. Michal, David's wife, was not among the celebrants. She was watching the procession from her window in the palace, and when she saw her leaping, dancing husband praising God, "she despised him in her heart" (2 Samuel 6:16b). When the celebration ended and David returned home to bless his own household, he was met with these chilling words from his wife: "How the king of Israel distinguished himself today! He uncovered himself today in the eyes of his servants' maids as one of the foolish ones shamelessly uncovers himself!" (2 Samuel 6:20).

David's uninhibited joy was genuine. He was not trying to make a spectacle of himself. It was not "the maids" he was baring himself before, but the Lord God Himself. David answered his wife as harshly as she had reproved him, and the Bible says that "Michal the daughter of Saul had no child to the day of her death" (2 Samuel 6:23). No doubt a subtle, but very real rift existed between the two of them from that point on. The sexual intimacy they once enjoyed in all probability ceased, never to be celebrated again.

2. An Unrealized Dream

Every man and woman must eventually face the reality that not all of their long-held dreams will come to pass. Some choices automatically eliminate other possibilities. Our own missteps place other dreams out of reach. God's plan supersedes our own. Soon after the incident with Michal, David learned that his fondest dream—building a house for God—would be denied. It was a goal he had kept in mind since early manhood. It seemed to him a worthy aim. But God said no.

God came to David's trusted spiritual advisor, Nathan, and instructed him to tell David not to build a permanent dwelling place for God. Although God promised David tremendous blessing (and although David praised God's decision even as it was revealed to him), a dream was nevertheless denied. Surely there was a strong element of sadness or disappointment at the news.

Please note that David's dream was not selfish or self-seeking or egotistical. He loved God and wanted to honor Him by building Him a house. But God had other plans: "When your days are complete and you lie down with your fathers, I will raise up your descendant after you, who will come forth from you, and I will establish his kingdom. He shall build a house for My name, and I will establish the throne of his kingdom forever" (2 Samuel

7:12–13). When David understood that he was not to be the builder of God's house, he turned his attention instead to military matters.

3. Worldly Success

Human logic would tell us that we are most susceptible to temptation when times are tough. Paradoxically, it is often when we're riding high that we're in true peril. David enjoyed tremendous success as a soldier and as a ruler. He defeated the armies of the Philistines and the Moabites, dedicating the spoils of war to the Lord. "David made a name for himself" (2 Samuel 8:13) as he "reigned over all Israel; and...administered justice and righteousness for all his people" (2 Samuel 8:15).

Perhaps David felt what a rising corporate star might who lands a big promotion or closes a great deal. Scientific studies have shown that testosterone (which regulates a man's sexual appetite) has been known to rise in nonhuman primates following social triumphs.[5] Consider Johnny Carson or Donald Trump, who both traded in aging wives for "younger models" following notable career successes. The multiwived J. Paul Getty once cynically said, "A long-lasting relationship with a woman is possible only if you are a business failure." Beware the intoxicating aura of success!

4. Loss of a Significant Relationship

David had suffered a rift in his relationship with his wife. He had endured the death of a dream and ridden the wave of worldly success. But perhaps nothing in his life was as difficult as the loss of his friendship with Jonathan, the son of Saul. David and Jonathan were blood brothers who swore lovingkindness (covenant loyalty) to one another in their youth. Sadly, because of the conflicts between David and Saul, that close relationship suffered, although their loyalty to one another remained until Jonathan's death and even beyond.

David and Jonathan were kindred spirits. They confided in each other. They held each other accountable. They were committed to each other's good. The loss of this intimate bond was evidently still fresh on David's heart following his great military triumphs. "Is there yet anyone left of the house of Saul," he asked, "that I may show him kindness for Jonathan's sake?" (2 Samuel 9:1). David was over-joyed to find a son of Jonathan, Mephibosheth, with whom he could share the blessings of God—and he provided for this young man, a cripple, for the rest of his life.

Still, the *phileo* (friendship) intimacy and accountability he had lost in Jonathan cost David. It may have even played a part in his tragic error of judgment. He had finally become king, true. But at what personal cost? He must have been learning just how lonely things could be at the top.

5. Disengagement from the Daily Grind

Finally, David's lapse into adultery came at a time when he had begun to disengage himself from the daily grind of ruling the nation of Israel. He was beginning to do less and delegate more. He was detached from the details of politics and battle, coming in at key points only. Second Samuel 10 gives an account of David's limited involvement in the war with the neighboring tribes of the Ammonites and the Arameans. He initially attempted a diplomatic alliance with them, but when that offer was rebuffed, he ordered his general Joab into battle on his behalf (2 Samuel 10:7). He came on the scene only to head the cleanup operation after most of the fighting was done.

Certainly many key leaders delegate important responsibilities as they should and must—but they understand they cannot ask others to go where they themselves have not gone. And "in the spring, at the time when kings go out to battle…David sent Joab and his ser-vants with him and all Israel…. But David stayed at Jerusalem" (2 Samuel 11:1). Was he depressed? Perhaps. Tired? Maybe. But he was a king whose country was at war, and instead of leading his army, he was lounging at home. He was disengaged from the daily grind of life—a fact that made him vulnerable to temptation in a way he might otherwise not have been.

A MOMENT OF MAYBE

The longer drama of King David's adultery was comprised of five things: a seemingly inconsequential rift, an unrealized dream, worldly success, loss of a significant relationship, and disengagement from the daily grind. These are still common today.

When the longer drama meets an immediate opportunity, we are faced with what has been aptly called a moment of maybe: "Even when a relationship is innocent, your friend may send the signal—or you may sense the feeling—of further possibility. It arises from a glance, a hug, a brushing of flesh that tingled more than you expected. An unspoken mutual understanding seems to establish itself. Perhaps you succeeded together in a project at work, and a greater closeness crept into your celebration. Perhaps one of you supported the other in a crisis; but the dependency became too personal. That's the moment of 'maybe.' In that moment nothing more is communicated than this: Our friendship could turn into something else. It is precisely here that the drama toward adultery begins."[6]

What happened to King David is tragically well-known. When other kings went out to battle, he stayed home. He got up from his bed early one evening and saw a beautiful woman bathing on a nearby rooftop. He inquired of others about her. He sent for her. He had his men take her from her home. He slept with her. She got pregnant. When he could not deceive her husband into thinking the child might be his, he had the man killed.

Where was David's moment of maybe? Novelist Roberta Kells Dorr, in *David and Bathsheba,* suggests it was his chance sighting of Bathsheba: "Bathsheba pulled off her shift and stepped into the alabaster bowl her servant Sarah had filled with fresh water. She stood naked in the bowl while her servant dipped water from a gourd and poured it over her. Bathsheba stood without embarrassment even though she had nothing to cover her nakedness. Unknown to her, a man's eyes had been observing, and ordinarily he would have turned away but it was all so unexpected and lovely that he continued to watch. With growing admiration, he studied her loveliness as only half seen through the dried palm branches. Her hair hung in damp curls to her full breasts and her tiny waist accentuated the pleasing roundness of her hips. As David watched, she stepped out of the bowl and tossed her hair back making the curve of her back visible. He thought he'd never seen anything so beautiful or graceful in his life. And he sent a servant and knocked on her door. And that evening, and that event which was to be a one-night stand, changed David and Bathsheba's life and their family's life forever."[7]

Now let's hear a modern version of this timeless story from a woman whose moment of maybe led her to the brink of disaster, although the relationship stopped just short of adultery.

I was married to someone whom I loved and who loved me. The possibility of having an affair or even coming close to one was never in my plan. So how was it that after twenty years of being a Christian and years of a fulfilling marriage, I found myself attracted to someone else?

He was married to my best friend and worked as my partner on a project that demanded a lot of time. We kidded a lot. Laughed a lot. Flirted with each other—innocently I guessed. But looking back, I clearly see that I completely ignored my instincts and common sense, thinking that I was immune. I wasn't. I also foolishly assumed that if I were happy in my marriage, I would never be interested or tempted.

I forgot the human element of greed, of wanting to be more, of having more, of the heady power that attention from another man can bring, of the carnal selfishness that this type of sin feeds and feeds.

For one thing, this person was handsome and I didn't consider myself anyone he'd be attracted to. That was probably number one. Then the instant I felt myself wanting to make time to see him when it wasn't necessary, I ignored this red flag. Rationalization was the order of the day. It was work. He made me laugh. I was sure his marriage and mine were okay, et cetera, et cetera.

Then one day he needed to make a trip for a presentation and asked me to go along. I didn't need to. And I didn't have to. I told myself that the strong instinct and attraction I felt was ridiculous and that he certainly wasn't looking for an affair. Looking back, once rationalization had set in, my ability to do more and more was staggering.

Analytically, the promise of more was more thrilling than any reality. The excitement and feelings of intensity were poor trade-offs for guilt, sin, deceit and shame. Today I look back and tremble for the mercy of God on my soul and on my marriage. What finally stopped this sin was the realization that it could go nowhere but deeper into danger. I grew tired of living with no peace and was sick with terror with the thought of discovery. Shame and humiliation were constant companions that I no longer wanted. And worst of all, perhaps on this side best of all, I wanted integrity again. I wanted to be free, cleansed, forgiven and restored. And I wanted my husband fully, cleanly, without the deceit hanging over me any longer.

Walking away from the situation was hell on one hand. Appetites of great power had to be killed. I wanted to know that Jesus Christ forgave me and made me clean and that He would still love me. I knew I had grieved His heart, but I know today that He was and is merciful beyond all human comprehension. Every time I look at my wonderful husband, I thank Jesus for His mercy.

Most people who play with this type of fire burn not only themselves, but their families and their church body as well. I am grateful for God's mercy and fully aware of how close to the precipice of destruction I came. For those who might think, "Well, you didn't go through enough, or pay enough," you are right on one hand. But the days of sick terror, sleepless nights and tears of shame were many before God. And on occasion I cry out to Him again, trembling with thankfulness.

I wonder how many married men and women could echo this person's story? Certainly more than you and I would guess. The truth is, adultery is democratic. It cuts across socio-economic lines, racial lines, religious lines. There is no single profile of an adulterer or potential adulterer. But there are some personal characteristics that may be common to those who break their marriage vows.

WHO CHEATS?

Those with unsatisfied appetites may cheat. When basic needs are not being met in marriage, the partners are more liable to affairs. Of course, we are all born with basic needs. Every baby that comes into the world is dependent on its parents for nurture. Those needs for approval, affection, and caring continue through childhood: "Daddy, how did I do?" "Mommy, will you come and kiss me good night?" "Can I have a drink of water?" "I'm hungry now." Babies. Children. Teenagers. Adults. All of us have needs.

When two people marry and promise "to have and to hold from this day forward, for better, for worse, for richer, for poorer, in sickness and in health until death do us part," they are saying to one another: "I am going to meet your basic needs until one of us is dead." What are those needs? Affection. Assurance. Companionship. Appreciation. Encouragement. Admiration. Sexual fulfillment. The failure of a husband or wife to seek to meet the needs of his or her spouse often leads to adultery.

Who else cheats in marriage? Adolescent adults cheat. Imagine that a couple goes in for marriage counseling and the husband confesses to numerous infidelities. The counselor, seeking to find out why the husband is unfaithful, begins to ask questions.

"Do you enjoy being together?"

"Oh, yes," they reply. "We have a lot of fun. He/she is my best friend, and we love to spend time together."

"That's good," the counselor responds. "But what about conflict? What kinds of things do the two of you argue about?"

"You know," they say, "we don't argue very much. We have so much in common that we seldom disagree over big things."

"Well," he continues, "what about your in-laws?"

"Oh, we love our families," they respond. "We try to get our folks together as often as we can. We have family reunions at our house every year, and we all get along just super. Our families were thrilled with our marriage from the beginning, and they've been very supportive through the years."

The counselor plays his next card. "Tell me about your children. Do they have any problems?"

"No," the couple says, "our children are great. They make good grades, they get along with each other, and they're popular in school. They've really got it together." Convinced that he's now isolated the problem, the counselor asks the couple to tell him about their sex life.

"It's wonderful," she says, and her husband enthusiastically agrees. "It's great. It just couldn't be more satisfying."

This is crazy, the counselor thinks. *I've got Ozzie and Harriet here. I'm interviewing June and Ward Cleaver.* Completely clueless, he looks at the husband. "If your marriage is so good," he says, "why are you having these affairs?"

The husband shakes his head. "I don't know, really. I guess it's just that 'forbidden fruit' thing. Other women are a challenge for me. I just do it because they're out there. There's something thrilling about doing what you're not supposed to do."

The couple's problem is simple: She has married an adolescent. He may be sixty, but emotionally, he's still in junior high. Sometimes grown men marry emotionally adolescent women too. A woman who has to constantly tease and flirt with other men to convince herself she's still as popular as she was in high school is an "adolescent adult," and adolescent adults cheat, sadly and tragically.

Finally, those who have unresolved conflict tend to cheat. Frustrated fighters who nurture running battles over housekeeping, in-laws, sex, household expenses, and hobbies are susceptible. Some friction in marriage is inevitable. Not only are men and women different, every individual is different. But when two people go through life not recognizing this fact and never dealing with their unresolved conflict, trouble is sure to arise.

TO THOSE WHO ARE CHEATING

Many who read this will say, "I recognize some (or all!) of the elements from David's life in my own: a rift with my mate, the loss of a dream, worldly success, relational loss, disengagement from the daily grind." Some will be able to identify their own "moment of maybe" where they surrendered to temptation and committed adultery. Still others, if they are honest, will say, "I am cheating on my mate right now. I'm physically and emotionally involved with another person." For all of these, I have a word of warning and a word of hope.

First, the warning. When you commit adultery, you are openly defying Almighty God and saying that His law is not applicable to you. You have chosen what is expedient or what is pleasurable over what is right. When you are unfaithful to your marriage vows, you are a "cosmic outlaw" before God, on the run from goodness and righteousness and peace. You are not safe.

If you continue in an adulterous relationship, that sin will take the very heart out of your life. Eventually, you will suffer the physical, emotional, and spiritual effects of your disobedience. It is inevitable because you are defying the true structure and nature of human relationships as designed by God. Even in a society that by and large excuses sexual infidelity, its consequences cannot be escaped. When Paul wrote that "the wages of sin is death" (Romans 6:23), he was precisely correct. Adultery is the devil's work and he does not pay well.

But I've got good news. The good news is that adultery is not the unpardonable sin. The good news is that God forgives. And forgets. And cleanses. First John 1:9 says that "if we confess our sins, he is faithful and just to forgive us our sins, and to cleanse us from all unrighteousness"(KJV). Only one who is Himself faithful and righteous can forgive and cleanse the unrighteous. And God alone is faithful and righteous.

Is your marriage in trouble? Here's what you do. Take off your boxing gloves. Call a cease-fire. Take a time-out. Don't respond to the bell of conflict by running to the middle of the ring with your gloves at the ready. Take them off and drop to your knees in your own corner of that ring. Then hear and take to heart the words of God: "'And I will be a father to you, and you shall be sons and daughters to Me,'" says the Lord Almighty" (2 Corinthians 6:18).

You can be reconciled to God through Jesus Christ, then reconciled to your mate as well.

Don't focus on what your mate has or has not done. Look at your own life and ask, "Lord Jesus Christ, what is wrong with *me?*" Then, in a spirit of humility and repentance, be reconciled with God. When you are right with Him, you are ready to move to the center of the ring and meet your mate. But don't run! Take small, baby steps. Go only as far as you can go without shouting, without malice, without condemnation. As you draw near to each other, ask God to administer His supernatural healing, cleansing, and forgiving. And listen as He whispers to you both, "Go and sin no more."

FAITHFUL ATTRACTION: HOW TO HAVE AN AFFAIR-PROOF MARRIAGE

Strangely enough, the first step to ensuring sexual fidelity in your marriage is to *admit the possibility* that either you or your mate could stray. Too many people, especially Christians, are convinced that they are bulletproof to temptation. No one is too old, too Christian, too happily married, or too moral to cheat. Why? Because every man and woman alive was born with a companion that never leaves their side: temptation. It was present on the day you were born, and it will be present on the day you die. That is why I know, without a doubt, that it is possible for any one of us to fall.

Who introduces temptation? The devil. And while the devil doesn't make anyone sin, he does tempt us with plenty of opportunities to sin. He is the evil one, the father of lies (John 8:44). Because you and I have physical bodies, he will attack us there. Because we are made sexual beings, we will certainly be tempted in all areas of sexuality. And because we are thinking beings, we will be tempted in our minds most of all.

Take particular care if you sense any of the following:

- You are just going through the "marriage motions" in your relationship with your mate.

- You are inventing excuses to see someone of the opposite sex.

- You are increasing contact with another in normal circumstances or environments.

- You are preoccupied with the thoughts of another.

- You are beginning to exchange gifts with a "friend" of the opposite sex.

- You are putting yourself in situations where a "friend" or "employee" might become something more.

- You long to touch, embrace, or continually gaze at someone of the opposite sex.

Any of these situations should put you on the alert. The first step in affair-proofing your marriage is to acknowledge that unfaithfulness is a possibility.

The second, closely related step, is to *expect temptation.* When temptation comes, don't be shocked or surprised. Temptations have come and will continue to come to each of us, in a variety of forms, sexual and otherwise. Don't make the mistake of thinking you are above being tempted; that is when the danger is greatest of all. "Let him who thinks he stands take heed lest he fall," the Bible says in 1 Corinthians 10:12.

Third, *do not be afraid* of temptation. God's Word promises that we will never be tempted by anything new or insurmountable. "No temptation has overtaken you but such as is common to man; and God is faithful, who will not allow you to be tempted beyond what you are able, but with the temptation will provide the way of escape also, that you may be able to endure it" (1 Corinthians 10:13). For those who are in Christ Jesus, there is a power available far greater than the lure of sin (see 1 John 4:4). The indwelling Christ is stronger than the forces of the world, and we must rely on His might when temptation comes.

It is not healthy to deny or fear the existence of random sexual thoughts or temptations. They are real. To acknowledge them is not to surrender to them, however. They should be recognized, but they must not be allowed to rule over us. Christian psychiatrist John White likens them to an unpredictable pet: "My sex desires are a God-given part of me. I do not need to be ashamed of them, guilty about them or afraid of them. But there are times when I must say to them, as I say to my dog, 'Lie down now....' Like my dog they may not want to obey. But they must be trained, and I must be the master."[8]

Finally, *guard your thought life.* Someone has said that our most important sexual organ is between our ears. The mind is the primary battleground of temptation, and it is there that we must apprehend every evil, lustful thought, bringing "into captivity every thought to the obedience of Christ" (2 Corinthians 10:5, KJV). We are not responsible for what comes to our mind, but we are responsible for what we allow to remain there. Proverbs reminds us, "As [a man] thinketh in his heart, so is he" (Proverbs 23:7, KJV).

Obsessively thinking of another person as a sexual object or fantasizing about a particular person or situation outside your marriage is dangerous business. Deadly business! "When lust has conceived," the Bible says, "it gives birth to sin; and when sin is accomplished, it brings forth death" (James 1:15). You and I cannot entertain sinful, lustful thoughts and hope to avoid sinful, lustful actions. Actions are the inevitable result of thoughts, just as birth is the inevitable result of conception.

But don't merely banish evil thoughts; replace them with good, godly thoughts. Let your mind dwell on "whatever is true, whatever is honorable, whatever is right, whatever is pure, whatever is lovely, whatever is of good repute" (Philippians 4:8). Determine now what you will do when temptation comes, as it certainly will. How will you conduct yourself at that convention...on that business trip...in the office...around friends of the opposite sex? Make up your mind today. And think often of the vows you have made before God and your mate and of the rewards of faithfulness.

DEVELOP A MARITAL SECURITY SYSTEM

Like many of our friends and neighbors, we have a security system in our home. When I open the door, I hear a little beep that reminds me to enter a code to temporarily deactivate the system. When we are in for the night, I enter the same code again so that an alarm sounds if an intruder enters. Why do people install security systems? So that they will feel safe in their homes and so that they can protect their loved ones and their property from those seeking to cause harm.

While every home may not need a security system, every marriage does! It takes a security system around every husband and every wife to ensure that a marriage remains intact, safe from those persons or forces that would harm it. Even if only one partner puts such a system in place, the odds of adultery occurring decrease by 50 percent!

One individual who is operating without restraints can wreak havoc in an institution, as proved by rogue trader Nicholas Leeson's single-handed destruction of one of Europe's oldest and most widely respected banks. Leeson, a twenty-eight-year-old trader with Baring PC, wiped out nearly a billion dollars in assets with a series of risky, unauthorized trades. A similar event took place several years ago at Merrill Lynch, causing that company to rebuild its safeguards from the bottom up, ensuring accountability at every level. Good safeguards are good business. Good safeguards also nurture good relationships—especially marriages.

A MARITAL SECURITY SYSTEM

1. Be Controlled by the Love of God

What are the elements of a good marital security system? First, both partners should be controlled by a genuine love of God. A key component of my own marital security system is that I really love God. I am astounded by His grace and mercy, His forgiveness, and the gift of His Son. It is something I've never really gotten over. It still amazes me. The Bible tells us that if we truly love God, we will keep His commandments (John 14:15). In other words, our obedience to God is a direct reflection of our love for Him (1 John 2:5–6), and only His love enables us to selflessly love our mate (1 John 4:19).

2. Be Wise in the Fear of God

Second, both partners should fear God. In fact, the Bible says that "the fear of the LORD is the beginning of wisdom" (Psalm 111:10). We are wise to fear Him because He is utterly just—taking into account not merely our actions, but the very intent of our heart. Some people have the idea that they can sin with impunity, that they can willingly and knowingly break God's commandments and still receive cheap forgiveness. But willing, determined disobedience, followed by a premeditated request for forgiveness, does not compute. God is no fool. To deliberately sin and then presume His forgiveness mocks His mercy.

Naturally, we all like to hear about God's grace and forgiveness, about second chances and beginning again. But that must be balanced with the understanding that, for the Christian, willful sin is a serious business. The writer of Hebrews says, "For if we go on sinning willfully after receiving the knowledge of the truth, there no longer remains a sacrifice for sins, but a certain terrifying expectation of judgment, and the fury of a fire which will consume the adversaries" (Hebrews 10:26–27).

Remember that under the Mosaic law, if two or three witnesses saw someone set aside that law, that person died without mercy. "How much severer punishment do you think he will deserve who has trampled under foot the Son of God and has regarded as unclean the blood of the covenant by which he was sanctified, and has insulted the Spirit of grace? For we know Him who said, 'Vengeance is mine, I will repay.' And again, 'The LORD will judge His people.' It is a terrifying thing to fall into the hands of the living God" (Hebrews 10:29–31). The fear of God is a part of my personal marital security system. I know that God is just and that He settles His accounts—not always in a day or even a decade—but He does indeed settle them.

3. Be Certain of the Judgment of God

In addition to the love of God and the fear of God, the knowledge that I will one day stand before God is a key component in keeping

my marriage pure and undefiled. One day you will stand before
Him too (Hebrews 9:27). Not in a group, or with an attorney, or
other witnesses, but _alone_. Each of us will stand before God individ-
ually and personally, and we will be held accountable for our
actions, our hearts, our minds, our motives. That restrains me. Does
it you?

4. Be Identified with the Cause of God

Long ago, seafaring ships flew flags that identified their vessel and its
loyalty to a certain king or cause. That way, approaching ships could
know immediately and from a distance whether another ship was
friendly or hostile. Flying that flag kept many a captain from mistak-
enly running from friends or inviting enemies aboard. I believe a lot
of marriages would be safer today if husbands and wives both "flew
the flag" of their commitment—to each other and to God—for all to
see.

Make it evident to friends, family, and foes alike that you are a
one-woman kind of man, or a one-man kind of woman. Make a
commitment now _never_ to spend personal time alone with someone
of the opposite sex who is not your spouse! As simple as this principle
is, it is a sure and tried protection against adultery. Why?
Because adultery rarely happens in a crowd.

If you want a secure marriage, fly your flag. Let it be known that
you are loyal to that wife or that husband. Let it be known that you
are a man or woman of God who holds marriage in the highest
regard and who will not cheapen your vows by infidelity. It is true
that you may "thin the ranks" around you by so doing—but you
will also provide a safer environment for your marriage to thrive and
grow.

5. Be Accountable to the People of God

Each one of us is accountable to God Himself. But the truth is, we
need "horizontal" accountability too: relationships with godly men
and women who will keep us honest and hold us to our word. This
is vitally important because we all have the ability to rationalize our

behavior and make costly errors in judgment, even when our intentions are right.

Only those who know us well are in a position to tell us when our attitudes and actions are straying beyond God's prescribed parameters. Being accountable means being willing to explain our actions, reveal our intent, and answer for our shortcomings. It means being vulnerable to a few who can be trusted to love us, affirm us, confront us, and most importantly, tell us the truth about ourselves. I am convinced that the simple safeguard of accountability could save many from sin—especially sexual sin. Chuck Swindoll writes, "Who can say how many Christians who have defected could have been rescued and restored had someone been honest enough to step in and assist them back to decency and godliness? Ideally, we would hope the person would want help...but not all do. Those who choose to be accountable have the greatest hope of change."[9]

6. Be Your Mate's Best Option

No matter what constraints are in place in your life, you cannot police the life of your mate in a way that completely ensures his or her faithfulness. You cannot always be with your mate, and you cannot set up twenty-four-hour surveillance. But there is something you can do to help your mate be faithful to you. You can make the grass on your own "marriage lawn" so rich and green that anything on the other side of the fence pales in comparison. By becoming your mate's very best option for companionship, for love, for lovemaking, and for nurture, you can extend that security system to your mate, as well.

When you give your wife or your husband affection, care, attention, praise, support, and encouragement, you are building a strong and compelling case for faithfulness. My aim in this regard is to so champion the life of my wife that no other man could come close to attracting her—and that is her aim where I am concerned as well. I can tell you for certain that nothing else could possibly measure up to her. I would be a fool to trade a Rolls Royce for a pair of roller skates—and I know it. By giving our mate our very best, we put another part of that marital security system in place. We make the grass in our own marriage lawn so green that any other option will appear to be blighted, brown, beetle-infested, and completely uncompelling—hardly worth a second thought and certainly not worth exploring.

7. Be Aware of the Deception of Satan

I am convinced that couples whose marital security system is strong can remain faithful to one another. But in addition to being controlled by the love of God, wise in the fear of God, certain of the judgment of God, identified with the cause of God, and accountable to the people of God, we need to be aware of the forces that fight against us. Deception is the enemy's greatest tool, and Satan must be pleased with seven myths that are prevalent today with regard to extramarital affairs. These myths parade about as truth, but each is false and unfounded. When you hear them, remind yourself that no matter who is speaking them and regardless of how forcefully they are spoken, they are completely, utterly wrong. Take it to the bank: Each one of these is a lie we must refuse to accept.

- *Everybody's doing it.* Yes, some are unfaithful, but many are not.

- *It's good for the relationship.* A breach of faith and the breaking of a covenant is never a good thing for any relationship.

- *You can't love your spouse and cheat.* Often the love of our spouse is not the issue at all. We can genuinely love our mate and yet walk into the trap of an affair.

- *It's the other spouse's fault.* This is blatantly untrue. If you are cheating on your mate, *you* have chosen to sin, no matter what your mate has (or has not) done. No adulterer is innocent.

- *An affair is strictly about sex.* Often physical attraction plays little, if any, role in an affair. Affairs are more about selfishness than sex.

- *Ignorance is bliss.* Pretending not to know if your mate is unfaithful is not healthy. It is never healthy to lie to ourselves. We must deal with reality, even if it is painful.

- *If an affair has taken place, the marriage is over.* The marriage may be damaged, but it certainly is not over. With time, attention, and care, the hurt can be healed, the damaged areas rebuilt, and the relationship restored.

CHOOSING TO LOVE YOUR MATE

The general state of marriage today is shaky, at best. At least half of all marital unions do not last until death. Serial marriage is becoming common. Unfaithfulness is no longer considered shocking.

But *you* can choose to hold your marriage in honor and to keep your marriage bed undefiled. *You* can choose faithfulness. Most affairs take place because people believe they can receive from another person that which they are not receiving from their mate.

A man strays because he believes somehow that he will find in this other woman what he is not finding at home with his wife (see the wisdom of Proverbs 5). Often that is sexual fulfillment—but not always. A woman strays because she hopes that another man will provide for her what her husband will not. Often that is affection—but not always.

Regardless of whether you have kept your marriage vows, you can make up your mind *today* to be faithful until death parts you and your mate. You can declare your commitment again. Regardless of whether you feel loving and affectionate toward your mate, you can choose to act in a loving, affectionate way toward him or her.

Love is a verb—it is a present and continuing action that can be expressed independently of feelings (see 1 Corinthians 13:4–7). Does that sound hypocritical? It is not! Sometimes we must love when we don't feel like loving. Such love is still real and still true. Too many of us believe that we must feel loving to act in a loving way. The truth is, loving actions can give birth to loving feelings.

Put a security system around yourself and your marriage. So love your husband or wife that he or she will not be tempted to look for greener grass in the arms of another. Love God. Fear Him. Fly the flag of your faithfulness to Him and to your mate—and fly it high.

And for those who may be in the midst of conflict over marital unfaithfulness, wondering whether it is worthwhile to rebuild what you once had, let me remind you that God is in the salvaging business. He never gives up on us. We are never out of His sight. He will answer every heartfelt cry of repentance with outstretched arms. You can begin again, with His grace, for He has promised, "I will make up to you for the years that the swarming locust has eaten.... And you shall have plenty to eat and be satisfied" (Joel 2:25a, 26a).

CHAPTER THREE

A Table for Two

How to Really Love Your Wife

N o one is as good at being a man as a man.
No one is as good at being a husband as a man.
No one is as good at being a father as a man.

There was a time when this was understood, but no more. Today the debate rages concerning masculinity and femininity and what it means to be male and female. Because we are sexual beings, our gender assignment influences everything we do. Our sense of ourselves as male or female begins in childhood, but as we grow into adulthood, inherent gender differences are often downplayed and sometimes even denied.

In one very critical sense, the sexes *are* equal: Men and women equally bear the image of God (Genesis 1:26–27). But that equality does not mean sameness. God has uniquely constructed men to be masculine and manly. And He has uniquely designed women to be feminine and womanly. This is not evidenced by what we do—it is simply what we are. The beautiful relationship between the two sexes—equal in standing before God but physically, emotionally, and psychologically different—lies at the root of marriage, the family, and society as well.

A study by Dr. Charles Winick at the City University of New

York examined more than two thousand cultures that have existed in world history and found only fifty-five in which masculinity and femininity were blurred. Not one of those unisexual societies survived for more than a few years. "Maleness and femaleness," writes Dr. James Dobson, "are not merely social niceties that have evolved through time.... The linkage between the sexes is a function of powerful forces deep within the human spirit. That attraction must not be tampered with by social engineers with an agenda of their own."[1]

God has programmed men to provide, teach, lead, and love. It is the man who provides a shoulder to cry on. It is the father's presence which makes everyone in the home feel safe. It is the man whom God has chosen for leadership in marriage and the home. The model is that of a leader, servant, and shepherd—not a CEO, dictator, or frustrated drill sergeant (Ephesians 5:21–6:4). In this context of marriage and home, a man is enabled to constructively harness his masculine energy and power in positive ways for himself, his wife, his family, and society at large.

All of this relates powerfully to the way that a man loves a woman, for if a man is truly confident and secure in his God-given manhood, he will be fully equipped to meet the relational needs of his wife.

THE FEAST OF MARRIED LOVEMAKING

If married love is a banquet, then the mutual sexual delight of a husband and a wife is a feast set out at a table for two. Listen as two married lovers celebrate their sexuality as if it were an exquisite meal. She: "He has brought me to his banquet hall, and his banner over me is love. Sustain me with raisin cakes, refresh me with apples, because I am lovesick. Let his left hand be under my head and his right hand embrace me" (Song of Solomon 2:4–6). And he: "I have come into my garden, my sister, my bride; I have gathered my myrrh along with my balsam. I have eaten my honeycomb and my honey; I have drunk my wine and my milk. Eat, friends; drink and imbibe deeply, O lovers" (Song of Solomon 5:1).

This is the way it was meant to be: a husband and a wife feasting on their sexuality and shamelessly glorying in the beauty of their lovemaking. But is it a realistic picture of the experience of most married couples, particularly Christian couples? Probably not. We've fallen far from this biblical ideal of married lovemaking. On the one hand, we are so bombarded with pseudoinstruction and "how-to" advice from our sex-saturated culture that we can't possibly hope to assimilate it all and measure up to the mythical standard.

wow

On the other hand, we are not quite certain how our spontaneous, uncensored sexual urges fit into the fabric of our Christian morality and can't help but wonder if physical passion is not somehow a competitor to our loyalty to Christ.

ditto

The truth is, God made us more-than-sexual beings. Sex alone will never satisfy us, but sexuality expressed within the framework of communion with each other and our Creator is utterly pleasing—to us and to Him. "God did not wince when Adam, in seeing Eve, was moved to get close to her," writes Christian professor Lewis Smedes. "Male and female were created sexual to be sexual together. When Adam and Eve...clung together in the soft grass of Eden, wild with erotic passion, and finally fulfilled their love, we may suppose that God looked on and smiled. Body-persons have a side to them that is wildly irrational, splendidly spontaneous, and beautifully sensuous. This is not a regrettable remnant of the beast in human beings...it is a gift that comes along with being body-persons."[2]

At one time sex roles were clearly defined and widely accepted, and the survival of a family relied on them. Choice or personal preference rarely came into play. Men did what it took to provide for their families. Women did what it took to nurture them. But in the last half-century or so, all of that has changed. Survival is no longer a matter of family interdependence. Broader options are available to both men and women. It is no longer necessary for a man and a woman to relate to one another as they have historically (and many do not). Departure from these traditional roles and values has made family life far more complex, multifaceted, and independent. Self-sacrifice for the good of others has been replaced by sacrificing others for self.

Moving beyond the singular issue of survival, husbands and wives are asking questions like, "Is there enough romance in our marriage? Is there good communication? Do we have mutual respect for one another? Are our individual goals being fulfilled? Can we have all of our dreams and still be devoted to meeting the emotional needs of our mate?"

There are new roles today and with them, new confusion—not to mention anger and resentment when expectations are not met. Sometimes men are angry, but more often, women are. Why are they angry? I'll tell you why. They are angry because men have treated them poorly, as a rule. Too many wives have been made to feel like a doormat for their husband's feet.

Husbands, here it is: The number one "marriage problem" in America (and therefore the number one sexual problem in marriage) is ungodly men. Most men once lived lives that were selfless and sacrificial before society and their families. Once they were committed, courageous, and compassionate. Today too many are selfish and self-centered. They have their own agenda and do their own thing, and in so doing, they cause the women who love them great pain.

FOUR DESTRUCTIVE HUSBANDS

There are four destructive personalities many husbands exhibit that prevent marriage from being what God intended it to be.[3] As we look at each one, consider the effect his personality could have on his mate and how his actions might impact her sexual response.

First, there is the *dictator.* His favorite scripture is Ephesians 5:22 ("wives submit..."), and he has never read much further than that. He likes the idea of a wife who is submissive to him, but he does not have a clue about what he is to be to her. Many times this man has what we call a "type-A" personality. He is a doer. A go-getter. He is probably choleric in temperament and prone to giving orders. Many times this man has been raised by an absentee father and, so by necessity, a dominating mother. To insure that no woman controls his life, he becomes a little Napoleon, a dictator.

One woman married to such a man announced, "I'm leaving my husband." I asked her why and was not surprised at her response: "I never make a single decision about what I wear, where we go, what our home looks like, or how we spend money. He runs everything and I am tired of being in prison."

This husband saw himself as a good provider. "How could you be unhappy?" he asked. "I've done all this for you to show you how much I love you."

But that was not love to her. To her it was total domination. It was life under the control of a mean-spirited descendant of Atilla the Hun!

Then there is the *powder puff husband*. He is passive, mild, and timid—and he doesn't dare rock the boat. Actor David Hyde-Pierce played this kind of husband to perfection in the hit television show *Frasier,* as hen-pecked Niles Crane, formerly married to the ever-invisible but formidable Maris.

Women fall in love with potential powder puff husbands because they are kind, sweet, and solicitous during courtship. But when this loving and gentle man becomes a husband who cannot make a decision, state an opinion, or take a stand, his wife quickly becomes disgusted with him, losing respect and admiration for him. For every dominating dictator, I've seen dozens of powder puff husbands. The son of one of these men was asked by a friend, "What does your dad do?"

"Oh, not much," the boy replied. "He just watches."

"What do you mean, 'he watches'?" the friend asked. "Is he a security guard or something?"

"No, he just watches. He watches me cut the grass and do my homework. He watches my brother rake leaves. He watches my mother cook supper, clean up the house, pay the bills, and take us to church. You know…he watches."

The man who just watches—the powder puff husband—is a destructive man. And his home is often in desperate, big-time trouble.

Then there is the *playboy husband*. Fed by a $5 billion a year pornography industry, men's clubs, and a user mentality, this husband is never satisfied, no matter how hard his wife tries to please him. He lives to "score" (even the word implies a game) and is always looking for the next conquest. He has role models too—professional athletes like Wilt Chamberlain and Magic Johnson—who have boasted of bedding thousands of women.

A man who indulges in this type of activity is destroying any hope of real intimacy with his wife and will eventually reap the tragic results of his promiscuity. Many who live by so-called "safe sex" also die by it and bring death to their family members in the process. This man is trouble, and the woman who is married to him is in grave danger.

Finally, there is the *driven husband*. Of all the destructive husbands mentioned here, he is the one most easily camouflaged in our culture. He is the company man, the career man, the achiever. Other wives may actually envy this mate and ask their own husbands, "Why can't you be more like him?" He may say he is doing it all for his family, but that is seldom the case. More often than not, he is feeding his own ego and seeking his own power or pleasure trip. His wife and children may be materially wealthy, but they are relationally poor. They have this man's name and his toys, but they don't have his heart—and they know it. Things are a sad substitute for the love of a husband or father.

Men, do you see yourselves? Ladies, do you see your husbands? In all likelihood, a man is a combination of two or more of these types, with some good qualities thrown in. But too many men are far from the biblical standard of what a husband should be. In fact, they would be hard-pressed to define or even to describe what that looks like.

THE JOB DESCRIPTION OF A GOOD HUSBAND

I believe that if a man truly seeks to be a godly husband and follows the guidelines the Bible provides for doing so, he will experience a dynamic marriage and a dynamic sex life. What is this job description? There are four key components.

First, he is to be a *provider*. In 1 Timothy 5:8, Paul writes that "if anyone does not provide for his own, and especially for those of his household, he has denied the faith, and is worse than an unbeliever." A husband is to provide. He is to be a worker. A producer. That is his God-ordained role in the family.

Second, he is to be a *teacher*. First Corinthians 14:35 says that wives who want to learn the truth of God should be able to find a ready teacher at home. The men of ancient Israel were urged by Moses to teach as well: "Only give heed to yourself and keep your soul diligently, lest you forget the things which your eyes have seen, and lest they depart from your heart all the days of your life; but make them known to your sons and your grandsons. Remember the day you stood before the LORD your God at Horeb, when the LORD said to me, 'Assemble the people to Me, that I may let them hear My words so they may learn to fear Me all the days they live on the earth, and that they may teach their children'" (Deuteronomy 4:9–10; see also 6:4–9).

We husbands are to teach not only by words, but by example, by precept. We are to model before our wives and children the kind of love and fidelity and openness and honesty that we would desire of them (see 1 Corinthians 11:1). We are to share with them the wisdom and riches of God, using our very lives as schoolbooks of instruction.

Third, we are to be *leaders.* "For the husband is the head of the wife, as Christ also is the head of the church, He Himself being the Savior of the body. But as the church is subject to Christ, so also the wives ought to be to their husbands in everything" (Ephesians 5:23–24). As is often the case, it is easier to demonstrate what something is not than to explain with words what it is. To see what leadership is not, let's go back to the garden of Eden.

Although Eve first ate of the tree of the knowledge of good and evil, it was Adam who was warned about its danger. In fact, God told Adam he was not to taste that particular fruit before Eve was even created! As far as we know, Eve never received a similar direct instruction from God, although Adam must have told her it was forbidden. Nevertheless, when Eve ate the fruit, she gave it to Adam and he ate too. But if Adam had been the spiritual leader, he would not only have refused the fruit, he would have tried to protect his wife from falling into sin. That was his responsibility.

Instead, when she ate and offered, he took—then compounded his guilt by blaming his wife. Notice that when God sought the guilty couple He did not call out to Eve, but to Adam: "Then the LORD God called to the *man,* and said to him, 'Where are you?'" (Genesis 3:9).

He placed primary responsibility for their fall squarely on the shoulders of Adam and then recognized Eve as his accomplice, a fact born out in the New Testament in the fifth chapter of Romans. Quite simply, Adam failed to be the spiritual leader God intended him to be.

Finally, the husband must be the *lover* of his wife and of the home. It would be so much easier on men if God left the interpretation of what it means to love our wives up to us, but He did not. He very pointedly illustrated what that kind of love should look like, and in no uncertain terms: "Husbands, love your wives, just as Christ also loved the church and gave Himself up for her; that He might sanctify her, having cleansed her by the washing of water with the word, that He might present to Himself the church in all her glory, having no spot or wrinkle or any such thing; but that she should be holy and blameless. So husbands ought also to love their own wives as their own bodies. He who loves his own wife loves himself" (Ephesians 5:25–28).

How are we to love our wives? As Jesus Christ loved the church. How was that? He loved her perfectly. He loved her sacrificially. When a man loves his wife without "spot or wrinkle or any such thing," he *makes* her beautiful. He sanctifies her, setting her apart to a special and unique position. When a woman is loved by her husband in this sacrificial and sensitive way, she will have a beauty, a radiance, a glow of joy about her that is unmistakable. There will be reverence, charisma, chemistry, and excitement in their relationship.

The man who seeks to be a provider, a teacher, a spiritual leader, and a lover to his wife is a wise husband indeed. But to do so in a way that truly says "I love you" to her, he must understand not only his biblical job description, but her basic needs.[4] And while all women are different, their most basic needs are almost universal. They are built in, and transcend age, social standing, and personality type.

A WIFE'S BASIC NEEDS

1. Nonsexual Affection

It seems strange to most men that nonsexual affection could be a key to a woman's sexual satisfaction. But it can. Too many men mistake a wife's need to be held as the cue to "make their move." She snuggles up next to him at the end of a long day, and he thinks, *Aha! Party time!* But she is thinking, *Hmmm…quiet time.* Or, *Time to talk.* This basic difference is why an amazing number of women believe in their hearts that they are married to a sex maniac, while an amazing number of men are convinced that they are married to a cold fish. The truth in most cases is that both are wrong.

Men, when your wife says, "Will you hold me?" chances are it has nothing to do with physical lovemaking—at least not at first. She really *does* just want you to hold her. That is part of the non-sexual affection she needs from you. You can also communicate it by complimenting her, praising her, and showing her understanding. Be affectionate, tender, and kind. (You must have been that way once, to win her!) Wives thrive on nonsexual affection, and wise husbands are glad to give it.

2. Open Communication

Women want to share with their husbands, and they want their husbands to share with them—honestly, candidly, and freely. They want open communication. This is tough for most men, who find it intimidating, or even hard work. A Roper survey found that 42 percent of women said "calling a friend" was relaxing to them. In contrast, only 27 percent of men felt this way.[5] Men, in contrast, tend to think and communicate like firemen. When you call the fire department and say, "There's a fire at my house," the fireman wants to know your address and the extent of the fire. That's it. Two specific, brief pieces of information, and he's off to save the day!

Women do not respond the same way. A woman would likely respond to a fire call with more than two questions. She might want to know if there was a lot of smoke, or if you had ever had a fire before. Perhaps she would even ask how hot you thought the fire might be, or if you were certain all pets were out of the house. And before you hung up, the odds are good that she would urge you to be careful and let you know how sorry she was that you were experiencing such a traumatic event.

Now, men—pay close attention. When your wife begins to share with you, she does not want you to tell her how to put out the fire or even matter-of-factly to solve whatever dilemma she is trying to sort through. She just wants you to listen! I know this is amazing, but it's true. If you could manage to ask her how she feels about it all, so much the better! She will let you know when she wants a solution. I am not made that way; neither are most men I know. But that is the way a woman is made, and we men need to turn off the fire hose and pay attention to her communication needs.

The typical couple spends only four minutes a day in "meaningful conversation." That is 0.3 percent of a twenty-four-hour day.[6] That is not enough. We must give more time for talking if our marriages are to be enjoyed rather than endured.

AN EQUATION FOR INTIMACY (SEXUAL AND OTHERWISE)

Men love equations. It just makes us feel good to know that something is going to work the same way every time. So here is an equation for intimacy that will go a long way toward making your marriage sizzle. Realizing that a wife's greatest needs are for non-sexual affection and open communication, what do you think the sum of these two things might equal? Their sum equals what every woman desires in her heart of hearts, even if she has not expressed it: security. *Nonsexual affection + open communication = security.* A man's willingness to give his wife plenty of nonsexual affection and open communication tells her that he loves her deeply and exclusively and that he will care for her needs as long as he lives.

A wife wants to know that her husband will love her as much when she is eighty as he did when she was eighteen. She wants to know that he will hang in there when times are tough and struggle with her to the very end. She wants to know that he will cry with her and rejoice with her. How does he assure her of all that? With affection and communication.

What does that have to do with sexual intimacy? Just this: For a woman, sexual intimacy flows out of a secure, loving relationship. "It is only in this environment that sexual experience can find the uncluttered trust...to grow into the adventure of sexual discovery.

Here, in the atmosphere of total acceptance, sex can be human and thus truly free. Sexual freedom is the liberty to explore the possibilities of sexual intimacy in the openness of trust, the security of unreserved acceptance, and the assurance of fidelity."[7]

Remember: *nonsexual affection + open communication = security.* If a man is having trouble listening to his wife, or taking the time to be affectionate with her in nonsexual ways, let me remind him that we men are natural hunters—and every hunter knows how to wait. A man will sit in a deer stand or a duck blind for hours in complete silence and stillness, waiting for the object of his hunt to wander into sight. If we can sit still for that, can we do any less for the precious object of our love?

WHAT IS SEXUAL INTIMACY?

Intimacy is the joy of two people coming together who are able to give and receive from one another. Sexual intimacy is the joy that is experienced when two lovers are able to give and receive freely with their bodies, their hearts, their minds, and their souls. Sexual intimacy with his wife should be the goal of every husband. What does this kind of mutual giving and receiving look like? Let me offer an example from two ancient lovers who no doubt experienced it. He was Solomon, king of Israel. She was his bride, the Shulammite. This is a record of their passion for one another:

> How beautiful you are, my darling, how beautiful you are! Your eyes are like doves behind your veil; your hair is like a flock of goats that have descended from Mount Gilead. Your teeth are like a flock of newly shorn ewes which have come up from their washing, all of which bear twins, and not one among them has lost her young. Your lips are like a scarlet thread, and your mouth is lovely. Your temples are like a slice of a pomegranate behind your veil. Your neck is like the tower of David built with rows of stones, on which are hung a thousand shields, all the round shields of the mighty men. Your two breasts are like two fawns, twins of a gazelle, which feed among the lilies. Until the cool of the day when the

shadows flee away, I will go my way to the mountain of myrrh and to the hill of frankincense. You are altogether beautiful, my darling, and there is no blemish in you. (Song of Solomon 4:1–7)

And the Shulammite's words of adoration to King Solomon are just as openly descriptive and passionate: "My beloved is dazzling and ruddy, outstanding among ten thousand. His head is like gold, pure gold; his locks are like clusters of dates, and black as a raven. His eyes are like doves, beside streams of water, bathed in milk, and reposed in their setting." She goes on to describe the object of her love from head to foot, and ends by declaring, "His appearance is like Lebanon, choice as the cedars. His mouth is full of sweetness, and he is wholly desirable. This is my beloved and this is my friend" (Song of Solomon 5:10–12, 15b–16).

These two lovers freely exchanged words of praise and uninhibited passion for one another. Their senses were "on tiptoe" where the other was concerned. They desired one another and did not try to hide that fact from their mate or from the world. The entire book of the Song of Solomon is alive with this kind of intimate interplay between a husband and his wife. It is one of the best "sex manuals" I know of. I recommend that you read it—in a modern translation if you dare—and learn how sexual intimacy is established and nurtured and enjoyed.

How Does Sexual Intimacy Develop?

One of the first principles we men need to understand in the development of sexual intimacy is that *sexual intimacy takes time*. This is true of a husband and wife's entire sexual relationship and of each sexual encounter. Sexual counselors Clifford and Joyce Penner advise newlyweds particularly that "becoming one—totally one—takes time. It takes time to mesh your worlds, communicate with one another, and delight in the stimulation of each other's body."[8] The progression of intimacy in the Song of Solomon beautifully illustrates this truth. When Solomon sees the Shulammite for the first time, he describes her only from the neck up. As their relationship moves toward marriage, he describes her body with more familiarity and detail, delighting in each revelation of his bride. After the two have been married for some time, the king describes his wife even more precisely and intimately, from the top of her head to the bottom of her feet, in beautiful, poetic, and sexually charged language. Not only does their physical intimacy increase, the depth of emotion expressed increases also.

A husband needs to remember this principle in each individual act of lovemaking. Sex therapist Dr. Douglas E. Rosenau advises that couples "take more time to enjoy each other sexually. Taking more time increases love play, and, in a fun way, forces you into being more creative. If ten minutes of mood setting and love play enhance sensuality, forty minutes may do four times as much. Time gives you the luxury of thinking about and enjoying sexuality in new and old ways."[9] Many therapists agree that *slow* is the operative word in great sex.

Timing is also crucial to the development of sexual intimacy between a husband and wife. Most couples seldom feel exactly the same way about sex at the same time, due in part to the differences in their physical and emotional makeup. Men have a tendency toward immediate gratification with focus on the genitals. Many women enjoy occasional quick, spontaneous encounters—but not as much as men. A woman for example, may not notice her husband getting out of the shower, but it is safe to say that if he is nearby, he notices her and appreciates the visual appeal of her naked body. Remember: Men are creatures of sight. They are moved by what they see. Women are creatures of sound. They are moved by what they hear and feel in their hearts.

It is important to note that the lovers in the Song of Solomon experienced this disparity in desire too. In chapter 5, Solomon approaches his wife for sex at what she considers an inconvenient time. "I have taken off my dress, how can I put it on again? I have washed my feet, how can I dirty them again?" (Song of Solomon 5:3). Solomon simply expresses his desire to her, and at the thought of his proposal, her feelings for him are aroused. "I arose to open to my beloved; and my hands dripped with myrrh, and my fingers with liquid myrrh, on the handles of the bolt. I opened to my beloved, but my beloved had turned away and had gone!" (Song of Solomon 5:5–6).

It was a matter of timing and a missed opportunity for sexual intimacy. The truth is, if couples waited until both felt equal sexual desire for one another, they would seldom make love. It is possible to choose to give your mate pleasure even when you are not in the mood—and like the Shulammite, you may find that your mood can quickly change! Husbands and wives should be open to some degree of sexual play with their mate, even if they do not particularly desire intercourse. "We can be turned on because we both *will* to discover each other's attractiveness and to make ourselves as attractive as we can. We may not ignite a fire of passion or erupt a volcano of desire, but we can at least will the way back to adequate love."[10]

Husbands, be sensitive to the issue of timing if you want to develop sexual intimacy with your mate. Schedule time for love-making. Don't give each other the "leftover" parts of your day. Be willing to go beyond your present mood to meet the emotional and physical needs of your wife, and remember to consistently and faithfully do the things that excited her when you were courting.

Also, sexual intimacy is developed through *timely communication*. Talk to one another about what you like, what feels good, what your sexual desires are. Verbalize your feelings for each other before, during, and after lovemaking. The lovers in Song of Solomon are constantly communicating with one another as they are making love. Many couples who love one another deeply never talk about sex together. They have never become comfortable doing so—or they feel they don't have the vocabulary to put their thoughts into words. Try to build a "love language" with your mate that allows you to verbalize your enjoyment of the sexual experience. And remember that anywhere from 65 to 95 percent of all communication is nonverbal. Touch, slight shifts of position or pressure, facial expression, eye contact—all of these can communicate to your mate in a timely and very intimate way.

Finally, *time away* builds sexual intimacy. The Shulammite plans a getaway with the king that would be hard for any man to refuse:

"Come, my beloved, let us go out into the country, let us spend the night in the villages. Let us rise early and go to the vineyards; let us see whether the vine has budded and its blossoms have opened, and whether the pomegranates have bloomed" (Song of Solomon 7:11–12). If Solomon was not particularly interested in horticulture, her final promise would have most certainly cinched the deal: "There I will give you my love."

What was she saying to her husband? "Let's go away and make love. I want to be all alone with you in a place that is for just the two of us." Husbands, your wife needs to hear these same words from you! How long has it been since you planned an escape that included the promise of a romantic, sensual time for you to experience the delights of married love? Sexual intimacy is nurtured and fed by time away...time together...time for two.

Husbands—how are you doing? If your love life is not what you want it to be, chances are good that it may be because you are not meeting the basic emotional, spiritual, and physical needs of the wife God has given you. What can you do about it? First, you can take full responsibility for your problem. That's right...*your* problem. If there is a problem in my marriage, it is my problem first, not my wife's.

I spent the first five years of married life trying to get Jo Beth to be more like me. I eventually came to the conclusion that my wife was untrainable. I was trying to train her to be like me and was convinced that I had married the only woman in the world who *couldn't* be like me. Three decades and some years later, I am thankful that we are as different as we are.

You see, as we said at the beginning of this chapter, men are men, and women are women. The sooner we move from denying that to accepting it, to celebrating it—the better off we will be! Men need to wake up and take responsibility for their own lives and their marriages. What is wrong in your life and your marriage is not your parents' fault, or society's fault, or even your wife's fault. It is simply *your responsibility.*

So how do you begin to change? By sincerely and humbly asking the Holy Spirit to identify the problem areas in your own life.

You can be sure that when you do, He will identify them clearly. When He does, repent. Say, "Lord, I recognize this shortcoming, this sin in my life—and I turn away from it. I repent." Begin to walk with God in dependence each day, asking Him to help you and guide you as you seek to become a man after His own heart and the husband that your wife desires. Then develop a strategy, a game plan, of very specific actions that you will take to communicate your love to your wife.

Sex is not the most important thing in a marriage. But it is a reliable barometer of the whole atmosphere of that relationship. If sex is to be dynamic, many other foundational things must be securely in place—so the state of your "table for two" can tell a lot about the state of your union. Great sex will permeate the atmosphere of your marriage and your home. When there is a deep and genuine sexual intimacy between husband and wife, there is fun, laughter, love, teasing, tenderness, adventure. Children will sense it, whether or not they can understand it! You can feel it. Your mate can feel it. It is like the aroma of a luscious banquet permeating every corner of your lives—and a wise husband will do everything in his power to ensure that it lingers, always.

CHAPTER FOUR

A Table for Two

How to Really Love
Your Husband

I was in a casual, general conversation with a friend when the talk suddenly turned serious. "I know you don't realize this," he said, "but I'm not happily married. My wife and I argue about one thing and one thing only—and that is sex. It's hard to believe that's what we argue about because we were so passionate when we were dating and looking forward to marriage. But that's the situation. We're at a standoff, and it's getting more and more tense and awkward every day." He talked a little while longer, then ended the conversation with these words: "I really don't know where to turn, but I can tell you one thing I know for certain: I do not think I can live the rest of my life in this kind of pressure-packed, almost sexless marriage."

I wish I could tell you that this man is a rare individual and that his circumstances are unique. But on the basis of my experience and the stacks of books and surveys I have read through the years, I know he is not. Statistics suggest that somewhere between 60 and 70 percent of all married men and women are frustrated to some degree with their sexual relationship. I believe that this is at least partly due to our culture's relentless blurring of the lines between true masculinity and true femininity.

Just as God programmed men to love, lead, and protect, He has programmed women to respect, respond, and nurture. Now before I risk the wrath of a generation of women, let me say again that the Bible's view of womanhood (and my own) is extremely high. I believe men and women are completely equal in standing before the Lord God. But again, equality does not mean sameness.

No one is as good at being a woman as a woman.

No one is as good at being a wife as a woman.

No one is as good at being a mother as a woman.

Only when a wife is comfortable in her God-given womanhood is she able to freely and completely love her husband and be for him all that he needs for her to be.

As different as men and women are—as different as God made us—we are still coming together and marrying, still having children and entering into the lifelong process of becoming what God has pronounced every husband and wife: one flesh.

Nearly a century ago, a noted essayist observed the phenomenon of marriage with more than a little humor: "The differences between a man and a woman are at the best so obstinate and exasperating that they practically cannot be got over unless there is an atmosphere of exaggerated tenderness and mutual interest. Every woman has to find out that her husband is a selfish beast, because every man is a selfish beast by the standard of women. But let her find out...while they are still in the story of 'Beauty and the Beast.' Every man has to find out that his wife is...sensitive to the point of madness: for every woman is mad by the masculine standard. But let him find out that she is mad while her madness is more worth considering than anyone else's sanity."[1]

The truth is, both our sameness (created in the image of God) and our differences (uniquely male and uniquely female) draw us together. We do not need to be more alike. We need to be more of what God created us to be as men and as women. I have already asserted that ungodly men are the number one relational problem, and thus, the number one sexual problem in marriage today. But ungodly wives—those whose actions and attitudes fall short of the biblical standard of womanhood—can damage marriages too.

FOUR DESTRUCTIVE WIVES

Consider then, how the personalities of these four wives might negatively influence their marriages and affect their husbands' sexual response.[2]

First is the *domineering wife*. This woman is in charge and calls the shots in her family, either outright or by coercion. She is choleric in her approach to life and typically marries a man she can control. The writer of Proverbs says that it is better to live in the corner of a rooftop than with this contentious, mean-spirited type of woman.

The domineering wife uses sex to assert her personality and manipulate her husband, either granting or withholding sexual intimacy depending on whether he has pleased her. He assumes the dependent role in the marital relationship—and she is dependent on his dependency. Domineering wives seek (and usually find) powder puff husbands, but such a union is not best for either of them.

The antithesis of the domineering wife is the *doormat wife*. This "Edith Bunker" type is usually married to a loser. Edith's sitcom mate was Archie—the prototypical caustic bigot whose pet name for his wife was "dingbat." The doormat wife is drawn to a man who treats her badly—and frequently sees in him redeeming qualities that are invisible to the rest of the world.

Many doormat wives were abused children or adolescents, and if they manage to survive one dictator husband, they may marry another, perpetuating the same vicious cycle. Their low self-esteem tells them they don't deserve better.

Then there is the *roller-coaster wife*. This destructive wife operates on the basis of feelings twenty-four hours a day, seven days a week. She can be funny and hilarious one day and in the depths of despair the next. Her husband never knows what he will find when he comes home—she may be swinging from the chandelier or crying on the floor. Lucille Ball played the ultimate roller-coaster wife on the old *I Love Lucy* show. Every day with Lucy was "like a box of chocolates." You never knew what you were going to get!

Finally there is the *independent wife*. She is married, but her life revolves around her own desires, her own needs, her own pride, her own interests. Her lifestyle is single even if her status is not. I know a lot of married couples who live independent lives. She has her domain...he has his. They don't have much in common but a last name and an address—and sometimes not even that.

It is impossible for the independent wife to experience the kind of "one flesh" intimacy marriage is designed for, because she is intent on maintaining her separateness. She wants life on her terms and sees her mate not as a partner, but as an accessory or an extension of herself.

Each of these four wives is destructive. The domineering wife, the doormat wife, the roller-coaster wife, and the independent wife have sabotaged marriages from the beginning of time and are still doing so today. I wonder how many wives—whether they recognize any of these destructive qualities in themselves or not—truly understand their intended role? The Bible gives a tremendous job description for a godly wife: how she is to live, what she is to do, and how she is to relate to her husband—even how she is to respond to him sexually.

THE JOB DESCRIPTION OF A GOOD WIFE

Following the principles that the Bible teaches about the role of the godly wife will orient a woman toward a thriving, vital marriage and an exciting sex life. In other words—God's way works, and His plan for a wife is all good! What are the attributes of this kind of godly wife?

First, *she loves and fears God.* She is devoted to Him and understands that her first responsibility is to Him. He is her primary source of strength, affirmation, and love. She relies on Him to meet her needs. Many times He can and does meet those needs through the life and leadership of her husband, but she understands that ultimately, God is her provider.

"Charm is deceitful," King Solomon advised, "and beauty is vain, but a woman who fears the LORD, she shall be praised" (Proverbs 31:30). Because this kind of woman is secure in the love and awe of God, she does not demand from her husband what only God can give: perfect, unconditional love. She knows that there is not a man alive who is able to be all that she needs, all of the time.

"It is simply not reasonable to expect a husband to have the perseverance of Prince Charming and Romeo, the mysteriously silent gallantry of Heathcliff and Clint Eastwood, the sexy brashness of Rhett Butler and Dennis Quaid, all the while unhesitatingly proffering comfort foods like a combination of the Keebler Elves and the Pillsbury Doughboy. The odds are that your husband won't both cook like Dom DeLuise and dance like Fred Astaire; it's rare to find a man who will show the compassion of Al Gore while exhibiting the wildness of Mel Gibson in *Mad Max*."[3] I would add that it's not rare—it's impossible!

Second, it is a wife's role to be *a helper to her husband*. She was created with this in mind: "Then the LORD God said, 'It is not good for the man to be alone; I will make him a helper suitable for him.' And the man gave names to all the cattle, and to the birds of the sky, and to every beast of the field, but for Adam there was not found a helper suitable for him. So the LORD God caused a deep sleep to fall upon the man, and he slept; then He took one of his ribs, and closed up the flesh at that place. And the LORD God fashioned into a woman the rib which He had taken from the man, and brought her to the man" (Genesis 2:18, 20–22).

A wife is to be her husband's colaborer in life—helping him in myriad ways to exercise dominion and rule over God's creation. How does she help? She helps him by being a trustworthy confidant: "An excellent wife, who can find? For her worth is far above jewels. The heart of her husband trusts in her, and he will have no lack of gain" (Proverbs 31:10–11). In other words, she is *for* him when the world is *against* him. She believes in him when others doubt. She listens to him and understands his heart. She is neither totally dependent on him, nor totally independent of him. Instead, she forges with him a healthy interdependence that reinforces their strengths and minimizes their weaknesses.

She also helps him by ably managing their household: "She looks for wool and flax, and works with her hands in delight. She is like merchant ships; she brings her food from afar. She rises also while it is still night, and gives food to her household, and portions to her maidens. She considers a field and buys it; from her earnings she plants a vineyard.... She senses that her gain is good; her lamp does not go out at night" (Proverbs 31:13–18). A wife's ability to manage the affairs of daily living is a tremendous blessing to her husband.

Third, a good wife *honors her husband*. She respects him and he knows it. This a direct instruction from God's Word: "Nevertheless let each individual among you also love his own wife even as himself; and let the wife see to it that she respect her husband" (Ephesians 5:33). A woman goes against the grain when she marries a man she cannot, or does not, respect. The fact that a husband needs and desires his wife's respect and admiration gives her tremendous power—a fact some wives never seem to comprehend.

How does a wife show honor to her husband? She listens to him. She speaks well of him to others. She refuses to share the intimacies or difficulties of their relationship with the world, but instead makes their marriage a "private oasis" where her husband knows he will be accepted and encouraged. Her honor is a magnet that draws him to her over and over again.

Finally, a wife is to be her husband's *best friend and lover*. Solomon's wife, the Shulammite, felt exactly this way about her king: "His mouth is full of sweetness, and he is wholly desirable. This is my beloved and this is my friend, O daughters of Jerusalem" (Song of Solomon 5:16). In marriage, the two roles—friend and lover—are combined in one person. "Marriage is to human relations what monotheism is to theology," writes Mike Mason. "It is a decision to put all the eggs in one basket, to go for broke, to bet all of the marbles."[4]

A godly wife is her husband's best friend, sharing his life side by side, and his lover, sharing his body and heart face to face. He desperately needs her to be both. "Men want more than just sex," says Dr. Archibald Hart. "They yearn for deep union of souls, a total harmony with another. They also long to open up emotionally, but they just don't know how to do it. They want their wives to understand that their sexual drives are stronger than women's and that they are not abnormal because of those drives."[5]

Many women fail to understand how closely a man's sense of

masculinity and self-esteem are tied to his success as a lover. "Making love is perhaps the primary means your husband uses to feel connected to you," Dr. Douglas Rosenau writes in *A Celebration of Sex*. "He may allow emotions to come out and himself to be physically close in a special way during your lovemaking. He also utilizes his sexual feelings to create variety and excitement in his life.... He has a different sexual reality from yours."[6]

The husband whose wife is his friend and who is assured that she enjoys their sexual relationship is a rich husband indeed. He looks to his wife to meet his sexual desires, and by fulfilling them, she affirms his manhood as nothing else can.

MUTUAL SUBMISSION AND DIVINE MARRIAGE MATH

Sexual intimacy takes place when a husband and wife are able to give and receive love freely with their bodies, hearts, minds, and souls. When a man and a woman marry, they agree to give their bodies to one another, exchanging individual ownership for mutual submission. The apostle Paul explains, "Let the husband fulfill his duty to his wife, and likewise also the wife to her husband. The wife does not have authority over her own body, but the husband does; and likewise also the husband does not have authority over his own body, but the wife does" (1 Corinthians 7:3–4).

Paul is talking about sex here! In God's design, sex and submission are inextricably intertwined. Unfortunately in many Christian churches and circles, submission has become the dreaded "S-word" for women. But it should not be. When a husband lives sacrificially before his wife and serves his family, and a wife submits to that servant leadership, it's not a struggle for either, but a thrilling adventure in obedience for both. "Who 'wins' this battle of wills and whims is not the point; the point is that each tries to surrender as much as possible for the sake of the other so that the love between them may be honored and built up in every way...."[7]

This mutual submission is also physical. A wife should give her body to her husband because she doesn't own it anymore—and a husband should give his body to his wife for the same reason! In marriage we are told that two become one flesh. In other words, one plus one equals…one. But in light of this Corinthian passage, it is also accurate to say that one plus one equals three, or four, or even more. What kind of math is that? It's divine marriage math!

A bow plus a violin equal not just the single sound they can make together, but the infinite variations of music their union can create. Edwin and Jo Beth equal not just "the Youngs," but the infinite possibilities of expression that our two lives can combine to make. This divine marriage math is made possible when we submit our bodies and ourselves to one another in loving obedience to God.

A HUSBAND'S BASIC NEEDS

It is important for every wife to understand not just her biblical job description, but her husband's basic needs. While every man is certainly a unique individual, collectively we have some basic needs that are nearly universal.

1. Acceptance and Appreciation

Men need, desire, and long for acceptance and appreciation. They especially desire it from their wives. There is not a man on the planet who is not driven by this need—a fact that gives tremendous power to the women who love them. The male drive to succeed, to conquer, to excel is made meaningful by the promise of any appreciative response those efforts might receive. A man's self-esteem is closely tied to performance, and we live in a culture that feeds that connection.

What does this mean in terms of sex? It means that a man wants his wife to accept and appreciate his sexuality. He wants her to understand the force of his sex drive and be glad that it is channeled toward her. Dr. Archibald Hart has said that many factors influence male sexual thinking. Among these are three behavior patterns associated with their sexual development: a) the tendency to repress their emotions; b) the tendency to be deprived of sensuality (hugging, kissing, touching, stroking, holding another close); and c) the tendency to be pressured to prove their masculinity through intercourse. "The fact is," said Hart, "that a man thinks about sex a lot, though it varies from day to day, depending on whether he has just had sex or not, on the level of his stress at work, and on other factors."[8]

Hart's study indicated that 80 percent of men think about sex at least daily, and some more frequently. The recent University of Chicago sex study reported 54 percent of men thought about sex daily—a number that caused humorist Dave Barry to conclude that "the other 46 percent of the men were lying. Because it's a known scientific fact that all men think about sex a minimum of all the time."[9]

Many women complain that their husbands are "obsessed" or "preoccupied" with sex, failing to understand that their sexuality is far more complicated than it appears on the surface. "Skill in lovemaking," writes marriage counselor Joseph Dillow, "is probably more intimately connected with a man's sense of masculine identity than a woman's skill is related to her feminine identity. A man can only establish his identity by doing something. The woman...receives her identity passively as her native biological functions mark her so clearly." That is why a man takes his wife's lack of acceptance or appreciation of his sexuality so personally. "When she doesn't express interest equal to his, he thinks she considers him a failure as a man."[10]

2. Intimate Connection

It might surprise many women to know that men also need and desire to connect with others on an intimate level. Most men want to know another deeply and to be deeply known—but they frequently lack the kind of communication skills that allow women to connect with seeming ease. Just as men tend to view sex as a means to "prove" their masculinity and success, they also see it as a primary means to achieve the closeness and nurturing they crave. Ask a married man who his best friend is, and he will likely say it's his wife. She, on the other hand, may have a network of caring, supporting, nurturing friends in addition to her husband. "To the extent that a human expression of love is the most powerful experience...that most of us encounter, man looks to woman as the vehicle for that expression."[11]

A man who feels lost or tired or angry may ask for sex when what he wants most is simply to connect in an intimate way with a caring partner. "What we experience in our own sexuality is a need for communion," writes Dr. Lewis Smedes, "...the biological experience is only the substratum of the whole sexual urge. What we want in sexual satisfaction is to be close to somebody, to share in the most intimate kind of exposure of ourselves, to give ourselves in spontaneous and uncontrolled trust to another."[12]

When a wife understands these needs of her husband, she will see how much of him is wrapped up in the act of lovemaking and understand that he is not only seeking physical release, but an affirmation of his manhood and a way to connect deeply with someone who affirms and appreciates him. When a woman sees that these male needs for acceptance and intimacy are often expressed through a man's sexual appetite, his strong sex drive becomes easier for her to understand and respond to positively.

FOUR ATTITUDES OF A SEXUALLY RESPONSIVE WIFE

Every husband longs for a partner who desires him sexually. He wants the woman he loves to want him—and in no uncertain terms. Unfortunately, many married men do not feel so desired by their wives and wish that the women they married could be more sexually responsive. A wife who develops the following four attitudes will assure her husband that she values their sexual relationship and enjoys intimacy with him.

1. A Positive Attitude

A sexually responsive wife has a positive attitude about lovemaking. Solomon's wife, the Shulammite, had pleasant, anticipatory sexual thoughts about her beloved: "May he kiss me with the kisses of his mouth! For your love is better than wine. Your oils have a pleasing fragrance, your name is like purified oil.... Draw me after you and let us run together!" (Song of Solomon 1:2–4). She was not fearful or apprehensive about their lovemaking, and she obviously did not view sex as something dirty or merely necessary. Some women may naturally have this positive expectancy, but others must erase old mental "tapes" to allow themselves to truly look forward to sex.

If your natural attitude toward sex with your mate is not positive, take some time to consider what negative messages you may have received in the past. What did your mother convey to you about the sexual relationship between a husband and wife? How did what you experienced in childhood, adolescence, or young adulthood shape your thinking? Which of those attitudes do you need to reexamine and alter to improve your sexual relationship with your mate?

Although girls are subtly taught to control their sexual impulses (and the responsibility of maintaining sexual control in dating relationships is too often left solely up to them), a wife needs to learn to cue in to her sexual desires and enjoy them. This positive attitude toward her own sexuality will be not only a source of pleasure to her, but a great turnon to her husband!

2. A Healthy Self-Image

A sexually responsive wife has a healthy self-image. I am convinced that more women would feel good about lovemaking if they felt good about themselves—and especially about their bodies. The Shulammite in the Song of Solomon described herself as "black but lovely" (Song of Solomon 1:5). Her physical appearance did not match the cultural standard of beauty for that day, but she realized her own unique attractiveness and was confident in it.

The media has done a number on too many women today who feel pressure to conform to a certain standard of beauty. A beautiful woman is one who is comfortable in her own skin, happy with her own unique features, and most importantly, radiant from within. Despite what women may believe, men are not nearly as likely to be critical of a woman's body as she is herself—and there is no one standard of physical attractiveness. "Please let go of the idea that there is any ideal body image that you have to measure up against. You can give and experience sexual pleasure regardless of body size or shape. You are worthwhile because God created you that way."[13]

Being ashamed of your body is a definite hindrance to satisfying sex. It is difficult to focus on the pleasure you are giving and receiving during lovemaking if you are self-conscious or embarrassed about your thighs or your stomach, or some aspect of your body that you deem less than perfect. By all means, if there is something that you want or need to change to be healthier and more at ease with your appearance, do it! But don't allow an obsessiveness about your body to inhibit your sexual relationship with your mate.

3. Uninhibited Initiative

A sexually responsive wife demonstrates uninhibited initiative at times. Those unfamiliar with the Bible would probably be surprised to discover that this kind of feminine initiative is scriptural! Solomon's bride let her husband know that she wanted him by arousing him visually: She danced for him and displayed her body in a provocative, alluring way. Did he take notice? You bet he did: "How beautiful are your feet in sandals, O prince's daughter! The curves of your hips are like jewels, the work of the hands of an artist. Your navel is like a round goblet...your belly is like a heap of wheat fenced about with lilies. Your two breasts are like two fawns.... Your neck is like a tower of ivory.... How beautiful and delightful you are, my love, with all your charms!" (Song of Solomon 7:1–4, 6).

She let her husband know she was interested in sex with him—and she did it through the gateway of his eyes! She realized that it was a compliment to her that her husband desired her and wanted to be with her sexually—and she turned the tables on him in an exciting way by saying with her dance, "I want you too." Wives, let your husbands know that you are interested in sex. Don't always wait for your mate to be the aggressor. Think about what he would like—and surprise him with it! If there is any sense of overwhelming modesty or shame lurking in your mind, do your best to overcome it.

And don't just show your husband that you want him; tell him too. Listen to the Shulammite's words: "Like an apple tree among the trees of the forest, so is my beloved among the young men. In his shade I took great delight and sat down, and his fruit was sweet to my taste.... Sustain me with raisin cakes, refresh me with apples, because I am lovesick. Let his left hand be under my head and his right hand embrace me" (Song of Solomon 2:3–6). She says clearly and with no apology that she desires him and even describes what she wants him to do.

I understand that for many women this goes against everything they have been taught and every preconceived notion they may have of what is womanly and right. But it's biblical. And either we are going to follow God's way and His plan for our lives and homes and marriages, or we are not. Wives, make up your minds to be creative in taking the initiative in lovemaking, at least some of the time, and see if your sexual relationship with your husband does not improve.

4. Enthusiastic Availability

Finally, a sexually responsive wife expresses an enthusiastic availability for lovemaking. Paul's admonition in 1 Corinthians 7:3 ("Let the husband fulfill his duty to his wife, and likewise also the wife to her husband") means that a husband and wife are to make their bodies available for one another's pleasure in a mutually submissive manner. I am not talking about intercourse on demand because it is your "duty," but about a flexible, open attitude that says, "I'm not on the same page with you right now, but let's take it slow and see what happens."

I'm convinced many wives would see their sexual relationships change for the better if their husbands believed they were more frequently available for sex. (And by the way, if husbands could expand their concept of sex beyond foreplay/intercourse/orgasm/ sleep, they would find their wives receptive more of the time.) The key is flexibility and sensitivity. No two individuals always want to eat at the same time or want the same meal. Likewise, a husband and wife will seldom want to make love exactly the same way at exactly the same time.

Differences in desire exist, but they can be overcome by the less-willing partner trading an "I'm just not in the mood" attitude for a "let's just try it and see what happens" approach. Likewise, a spouse whose partner is not in the mood for sex should be willing to adapt his or her expectations: "When sex means 'do something for me because I want it whether you feel like it or not,' it's not very appealing," writes one sex therapist. "But when sex means 'let me hold you and affirm you and touch you in any way you wish,' a refusal is less likely."[14]

For wives who are convinced that if they were any more sexually available they would never get out of bed, let me offer this analogy. A child whose parent responds to most requests with an automatic no will ask almost constantly for the thing he desires—whether it is ice cream or an afternoon of swimming—hoping for an eventual yes. But if the parent has proven that he considers all reasonable requests, (and takes great joy in saying yes), the child is compelled to ask less frequently, assured that when he does he is likely to be satisfied. As often as you can, make your response to your husband's sexual overtures positive. And be flexible! You will find that an attitude of enthusiastic availability means the world to the husband who desires his wife.

Wives, how are you doing? Is the sexual relationship between you and your husband a true feast, a beautiful, intimate table for two? Or is it a standoff, a guessing game, or a source of conflict and irritation? Night after night, in city after city and home after home, the same scene is being played out in countless bedrooms. A husband and wife undress and climb into bed, turning out the lights. They lay side by side, separated only by inches perhaps—but in reality, miles apart. A word is said, a touch is offered, and a message comes back, verbally or nonverbally, that tonight is not the night. They haven't connected. They haven't communicated. And there is a coldness, an ache, a wonderment in a husband's heart—or a wife's. *I wonder what it would be like,* they think, *to be married to someone who really desired me...who wanted to make love to me?*

Is that your house? Your marriage? Your bed? It doesn't have to be—and it certainly wasn't meant to be. God created a banquet for every man and wife. The invitations are issued. The table is set. Come and dine. "Eat, friends; drink and imbibe deeply, O lovers" (Song of Solomon 5:1).

CHAPTER FIVE

Pure Lovemaking

Marital Intimacy by the Book

The duality, the separateness of body and spirit, is not found in the Bible. It is Platonic philosophy that makes the body/spirit distinction, on the premise that the physical cannot be spiritual and the spiritual cannot be physical. Scripture teaches, in contrast, that true spirituality embraces all of what it means to be human, including sex.

The Bible's reference to the church as the "bride of Christ" is powerful and vivid symbolism. Sexual oneness between a husband and a wife is like the oneness between God and His people. Sex—pure sex, real sex—apart from Him is impossible!

It should come as no surprise, then, that making love is one of the most exciting and exhilarating experiences in life. When we make love according to God's design, not only can we enjoy incredible physical satisfaction, but great spiritual, psychological, and emotional pleasure as well.

Why? Because sex was God's idea. He created it as a marvelous gift for man and woman to celebrate within the marriage relationship. Great lovemaking is *pure*. It is untainted by sin or guilt or deception or fear or selfishness. Sexual expression that conforms to the wise parameters set forth in God's Word, the Bible, is pure lovemaking…and pure lovemaking should be the goal of every husband and wife.

Would you like to experience that kind of lovemaking? Then let me direct you to what is perhaps one of the most beautiful, lyrical passages in the New Testament: 1 Corinthians 13. It is often called "the love chapter," and it describes a love that is to be cultivated in all areas of life. But when it is applied to husbands and wives, and specifically to the act of making love, I believe the merely ordinary can become extraordinary indeed.

First, consider these inspired words from the apostle Paul: "If I speak in the tongues of men and of angels, but have not love, I am only a resounding gong or a clanging cymbal. If I have the gift of prophecy and can fathom all mysteries and all knowledge, and if I have a faith that can move mountains, but have not love, I am nothing…. Love is patient, love is kind. It does not envy, it does not boast, it is not proud. It is not rude, it is not self-seeking, it is not easily angered, it keeps no record of wrongs. Love does not delight in evil but rejoices with the truth. It always protects, always trusts, always hopes, always perseveres. Love never fails…. And now these three remain: faith, hope and love. But the greatest of these is love" (1 Corinthians 13:1–8, 13, NIV).

No less than nine times in this writing, Paul will use the wonderful word *agape* to describe the kind of love that we are to demonstrate to one another. *Agape* speaks of a love that is volitional, not merely emotional. It is a love rooted in the will. A choice. In contrast, *eros*, the most common Greek word of that day for love, is never found in the New Testament. *Eros*—physical attraction and desire—certainly has a place in married lovemaking. In fact, God applauds it as necessary, healthy, and essential; but it is not adequate to describe the self-sacrificing, unconditional love that is our ideal.

Philos is another Greek word for love that means brotherly affection and esteem. Again, *philos* is important to a marriage relationship, but it is not the key ingredient in married love.

Certainly the lovers in the Song of Solomon displayed *eros* and *philos* to one another, and the Song itself indicates that God applauds emotional, sensual, and erotic love. But if a marriage is to be all that He intends it to be, *agape* must be its overarching theme. In this kind of love, husband and wife both seek the other's highest good. *Agape* lovers are more interested in their mate's pleasure and well-being than in their own. What does this love look like when it's put into practice? The apostle Paul describes two primary characteristics of *agape* in 1 Corinthians 13.

AGAPE LOVE IS ESSENTIAL

"If I speak in the tongues of men and of angels, but have not love, I am only a resounding gong or a clanging cymbal. If I have the gift of prophecy and can fathom all mysteries and all knowledge…but have not love, I am nothing. If I give all I possess to the poor and surrender my body to the flames, but have not love, I gain nothing" (1 Corinthians 13:1–3, NIV).

Words, knowledge, and noble actions are no substitute for *agape* love. It is essential. All else is secondary. Without this kind of love, it does not really matter what we say or how beautifully we say it. Without *agape,* lovely words and well-chosen phrases eventually become annoying; they are like a "resounding gong or a clanging cymbal." (Paul must have piqued the pride of many religious leaders of the day by comparing their loveless discourses to the noises made by pagan instruments!)

Without this *agape* love, Paul said it does not matter what we know. People blessed with the Christian gifts of prophecy, discernment, and understanding, but lacking in *agape* are nothing in God's estimation. They are a zero. Knowledge without love does not build up, it only puffs up.

Perhaps most shocking of all, without *agape* love, it does not even matter what we do. According to Paul, acts of service—like giving all of one's possessions to the poor, or acts of sacrifice like surrendering one's very body to be burned (and Rome was burning plenty of Christians as the apostle wrote)—were worthless if they did not spring from *agape.*

Now, do not misunderstand. Paul was not saying that what we say, what we know, and what we do never matter. He simply argued that without love—*agape* love—our words lack impact, our knowledge is pointless, and our good deeds are hollow and empty.

What does this mean in terms of married lovemaking? It means that a man may be very persuasive with his words, but if his wife does not believe they come from a selfless, loving heart, she will not be won by them. She will not desire intimacy with a man who merely speaks empty words. It is impossible to know one another deeply, sharing our innermost thoughts and feelings (something that is essential to a meaningful and successful sex life), if we do not believe that our spouse loves us unconditionally.

Without *agape*, we will fear disclosure, and our knowledge of one another will be limited. We may even lavish gifts on one another and do sweet things for each other, but if our mates do not believe that our actions are backed up by love, they will probably feel like we are trying to buy them off. Without *agape*, the sex act which God intended to be beautiful and wonderful becomes manipulative and hurtful. That is why *agape* love is essential to pure lovemaking.

AGAPE LOVE IS EXPRESSIVE

In this Corinthian letter, Paul uses twelve descriptive phrases to portray Christlike, *agape* love. All of them describe love in action—love *doing* something. They are all in the present tense, indicating they are to be continuing actions. These are not things we are to do once, or even occasionally, but rather they are to be taking place in our lives continually and consistently.

Paul is not describing a perfect state of being, but an ongoing state of development. No husband and wife will exhibit all of these characteristics all of the time, but they can (and should!) be moving closer and closer to the ideal every day. Applied to the act of lovemaking, these twelve things can be truly life-changing!

1. Love Is Patient

Unfortunately, we men are less prone to exercise patience sexually than our wives are. To put it bluntly, too many men are in a hurry when it comes to lovemaking. The natural male tendency is to see sex as a race with orgasm (his own) as the finish line. But the man who loves his wife as he should will be slow and patient, spending ample time in foreplay and prolonging her pleasure.

A man needs to understand that his actions are far more critical to his wife's satisfaction than hers are to him. That is, men (almost without exception) *will* have an orgasm during intercourse. Women, on the other hand, are more dependent on their husband's cooperative actions to reach a climax. A man who is patient and attentive in lovemaking, allowing his wife the time she needs to experience complete arousal and orgasm, will find himself becoming irresistible to her.

2. Love Is Kind

Our lovemaking needs to be gentle, caring, and affectionate. Both words and actions can convey this pervading atmosphere of kindness. A wife is motivated to love her husband in a satisfying way when she understands how much her enthusiastic response means to his self-esteem and emotional well-being. She provides the confidence that is necessary for him to "do battle" in his world and to be a romantic lover in his home. A husband is motivated to love his wife in a satisfying way when he understands how his loving words and affectionate touches give her a sense of security—especially when they are offered outside of the bedroom!

Kindness also involves sensitivity in touch during lovemaking. Women's bodies are more tender than usual at certain times, making rough caresses, rapid entry, and deep thrusting painful, rather than exciting. A few words of understanding and direction at the beginning of a sexual encounter can prevent unnecessary discomfort or disappointment.

3. Love Does Not Envy

That love does not envy means it does not want what others have. In our body-obsessed, performance-oriented society, this is especially applicable. Too many men and women have an inferiority complex where their bodies and sexual responses are concerned. If men/women believe they are inadequate lovers, they usually will be.

The good news for those of us in Christ is that we are wholly acceptable and completely loved, as is, in God's sight! For this reason, we can legitimately feel good about ourselves as sexual beings. Instead of envying the bodies or perceived sensuality of others, we can rejoice in our own uniqueness, taking whatever steps are reasonable to develop into the kind of lover that will more fully meet the needs of our mate—not the standards of our narcissistic culture.

4. Love Is Not Boastful or Proud

Some spouses act as if their partners are fortunate to have the privilege of making love to them, approaching the bedroom as if they were God's gift to the world, and to their mate. This can only be repulsive and disheartening to their wife or husband. Lovemaking is not about parading around or performing. It is about serving one another. It is about cherishing and nourishing one's partner.

A real man most fully enjoys his masculinity when he knows he has pleased and satisfied his partner. A real woman truly delights in her femininity when she makes it her goal to please and satisfy the husband God has given her. Great lovers not only communicate what they themselves find pleasing, but they seek to discover what pleases their mate too.

5. Love Is Not Rude

Love is not rude; it is sensitive. Here again, many men fall short. A woman is seldom turned on by a man's sweaty, smelly body. She wants to be near someone who looks good, smells good, and tastes good—and who is sensitive to her feelings and preferences. Few women enjoy having a man's day-old beard rubbed against their face or breasts, or any other part of the body. A sensitive husband will consider how his wife feels about these things and act accordingly. Beyond his attentiveness to the physical aspects of lovemaking, a loving husband will take care with his words as well, knowing that thoughtless or insensitive remarks can hurt his mate deeply.

Women, too, need to consider how half-hearted responses and ill-timed, negative comments during lovemaking might be hurtful to their husbands. A woman who refuses to move or to touch her husband during sex, or who cuts him off with a harsh, negative word is not being sensitive to his feelings. But if she understands that there are times he needs her to be the pursuer, to take the initiative, and to express desire for him, his self-esteem and enthusiasm will soar.

6. Love Is Not Easily Angered

There is no place for a short fuse in lovemaking and no place for keeping a record book of offenses (real or imagined) committed by one's spouse. Even in times when there is sexual confusion and mis-communication (and there will be), we must be quick to seek one another's forgiveness. Bitterness is a cancer to the soul and a barrier to the act of pure lovemaking. It can consume our thoughts and color our entire outlook on life.

For sex to be all that it can and should be, bitterness between a husband and wife must never be allowed to take root. Offenses must be confessed and reconciled in a timely way, and we must truly and genuinely put behind us any hurts that would mar the wonderful expression of love that God has given us.

7. Love Does Not Rejoice in Iniquity

Real love, *agape,* rejoices in the truth. Love seeks complete honesty and open communication. Most therapists say that sexually dysfunc-tional couples do not talk to one another. The man does not know what pleases his wife. The wife does not know what pleases her hus-band. It is critical that we talk about the things we enjoy in love-making. We must communicate to our mates the things that excite us and bring us pleasure: when we want to be touched; how we want to be touched; where our most sensitive touch points are; what kinds of caresses and kisses excite and thrill us.

Because love rejoices in the truth, it is never loving to lie about sexual response. Many women have been led to believe that faking orgasm, or lying about whether or not they were satisfied, is kinder or more acceptable than telling the truth. In the long run, it is not. Although a wife may be motivated out of love for her husband, not wishing to disappoint him or cause him to feel inadequate, she needs to be honest about when she reaches orgasm and when she does not—and this truthfulness must be met without resentment.

Love rejoices in the truth. In lovemaking, a husband and wife must be truthful about their shared experience and so grow and learn together.

8. Love Bears All Things

The protective nature of *agape* love prohibits a spouse from insisting his or her mate do anything sexually they find painful or distasteful. While virtually any activity that a husband and wife deem mutually pleasing and safe is acceptable in marriage, what may be good and right for one couple will not be for another. The issue is not "what are *other* couples doing?" but "what are we going to do to express our love and meet our sexual needs in a way that is healthy and satisfying for us both?"

Simply put, a husband should never badger his wife to do anything that is hurtful or distasteful to her, and a wife should never demand from her husband any sexual expression he finds uncomfortable or unpleasant. One word of caution is in order: Do not let your protection of each other's feelings become a barrier against asking or experimenting. Trying new things (even if you both end up laughing), or reprising old experiences (how long has it been since you've gone parking in a secluded spot?) can keep your lovemaking from becoming routine and predictable.

9. Love Believes All Things

It is the nature of *agape* love to believe. *Agape* lovers believe not only the best about their beloved, but the best about their love itself. Their wholehearted commitment to each other sends a message to the outside world while it reinforces their oneness. Amazing things happen in a marriage when a husband communicates to his wife that he is a one-woman man and that she is that one woman. Likewise, a woman who communicates to her husband that she is in love with and sold out to only one man, and that he is that man, will reap the benefits of trust and freedom that her assurance brings.

When a couple believe wholeheartedly in one another and in their union in this way, every act of lovemaking becomes a new affirmation of their covenant, a reciting of their "creed," and a celebration of their own unique partnership. And perhaps best of all, belief is contagious—giving those around them a sense that such a union might be possible for them too!

10. Love Hopes All Things

Agape love is optimistic. It is encouraging. It does not believe that the best is over, but that the best is up ahead. When Jo Beth and I married, her uncle Wilfred quoted these words of Browning at our wedding: "Grow old along with me! / The best is yet to be, / The last of life, for which the first was made. / Our times are in his hand / Who saith, 'A whole I planned; / Youth shows but half. Trust God; see all, nor be afraid!'" They have turned out to be true.

Thirty-seven years, three sons and five grandchildren later, I am convinced that the best for my wife and me—even sexually—is not in the past. It is somewhere in the future. Why? Because *agape* love hopes all things. And the hope described here is not simply wishful thinking. It is "robust, vigorous confidence built on the fact that God is holy love."[1]

I have honestly found that the sexual dimension of life is better now than it has ever been. With age have come a greater under-standing, a greater sensitivity, and a greater love. As thrilling as those early days of marriage were, the love and intimacy that my wife and I now share is greater still. Love believes the best days are still ahead.

11. Love Perseveres

Perhaps the most tender aspect of *agape* love is that it perseveres. It keeps on loving no matter what. Any couple can experience a fleet-ing sexual "high" or a season where lovemaking seems electric and effortless—but to keep sex alive, vital, and interesting through the years is the mark of *agape*. *Agape* lovers continue to give themselves to one another in lovemaking through times of illness, job stress, infertility, parenthood, conflict, grief, loss, change, and even unmet expectations.

During the difficult (or less than thrilling) times, lovers who persevere will discover that the love they have made—physically, emotionally, and spiritually—can carry them over the rough spots.

"Perhaps the ultimate test," writes Mike Mason, "will be in whether or not they can believe in those times of almost perfect giving and acceptance, never doubting or resenting or forgetting them afterwards in the stress of trial and daily life, but rather building on them, taking them as the models of what their love must be...nurturing and enlarging those deep seeds of intimacy that have been so lovingly planted in the memory of their flesh."[2]

12. Agape Love Is Enduring

The final characteristic of *agape* love is that it is enduring. "Love never fails," Paul writes, and by that he means that love always wins and never loses. Even when we love sacrificially and selflessly but find our love is rejected, love endures. Poet Luci Shaw says, "The real treasures do not vanish. The precious loses no value in the spending.... A piece of hope spins out bright, along the dark, and is not lost in space.... Love is out orbiting, *and will come home.*" How do I know that *agape* love endures? Because the Bible teaches that God is love (1 John 4:8) and that He is eternal—from everlasting to everlasting.

If He is love and He is eternal, then His people—empowered by His spirit—can and should love one another throughout this life and beyond. That is why Paul can say with confidence, "But now abide faith, hope, love, these three; but the greatest of these is love" (1 Corinthians 13:13). Faith will one day give way to sight. Hope will one day give way to reality. But love, well...it will just keep on going forever.

Husbands and wives who give to one another the kind of *agape* love described in 1 Corinthians 13 are certain to find the joy and thrill that God designed in lovemaking from the very beginning. Only when you and I make love God's way—by His book—will we experience the kind of pure lovemaking that is sex at its very best.

CHAPTER SIX

"Where Did I Come From?"

Teaching Children

about Pure Sex

I t is only a matter of time before each one of us hears the five most terrifying words in the English language. Do you know what they are? Not, "Your test results are in," delivered by a physician; or, "There has been an accident," spoken by a stranger; or even, "The Internal Revenue Service called," mentioned off-handedly by someone in the office. No, I daresay that for any parent the most terrifying words we will ever hear are these, spoken by a child: "Mommy (or Daddy), where did I come from?"

Maybe you remember asking these words yourself as a child, or struggling for just the right response when your children asked them of you. As a parent myself, I can tell you that when these words are spoken, something happens to the bravest of us all. We are seldom completely at ease and prepared. When it comes to explaining the facts of life, we fumble more often than we would like to admit.

So what *do* we tell our children when the tough questions come? Here are a few of what I believe are typical responses from folks who were asked, "Who told you about sex, and what did they say?"

I asked my dad where babies come from, and he went into this long explanation about mares and stallions. I remember thinking, *What does this have to do with anything?* Then when he finished he said, "Don't tell Billy [my best friend] what I just told you. His dad will tell him."

My mom told me about sex in the fourth grade. My dad was in the room, but he didn't say much. It was all really vague and confusing. She kept talking about animals, and avoiding words she didn't want to say—but somehow wanted me to understand. My dad's only comment was, "You know, son, it's like when we go out to the farm and you see the cows and bulls together. That's what it's all about." When I walked out of there I was totally confused. It left a lot more questions than it gave answers, that's for sure.

I learned about the birds and the bees in school...in sex education class. I didn't ever talk to my parents about it. I learned nothing about the emotional part of sex, or about morality—just about how all the parts work. I felt uncomfortable because my family never talked about it. It was awkward.

I honestly don't remember anyone sitting me down and talking to me about sex. The things I learned were from school and from friends. If my parents said anything, I don't remember it. The only thing I vividly recall was this really fast girl in high school—she was a sophomore—telling me what intercourse was. I was just shocked.

But perhaps my favorite story is the one told by a young lady who made her mom the "Dr. Ruth" of their neighborhood: "My mom got a book from our pediatrician, thinking it would be better if we knew a few facts before we sat down to talk. My brother and I read the book at the same time. My dad talked to my brother and my mom talked to me, going over everything I'd read and asking if I understood or had any questions. Then about the same time, in school, they showed 'the films.' All the kids in the neighborhood started talking about what we'd seen, and whenever they would ask questions I would say, 'I don't know—but come on over to my house, because my mom knows everything about sex and she'll know the answer for sure!'"

These fateful episodes were recalled by individuals now twenty to forty years old—but when it comes to talking to our children about sex, I'm not sure that we parents have improved our content or delivery much in recent years. One thing has changed, though. Today, regardless of whether children are receiving any kind of sex education at home, they *are* getting it elsewhere—either in the form of Contemporary Sex Education (CSE) at school, or from their peers, television, movies, music, etc.

No matter how we might struggle to answer the tough questions, our attempts to field them are generally well intended and seldom harmful. The same cannot always be said for other sources of sex information. You can be sure of this: If we do not answer our children's questions about sex, someone else will. And we cannot be certain of either the intent or integrity of the answers given by the media, our children's peers, or their teachers. In fact, with the misinformation bombarding young people today, parents *must* do more than feebly attempt to provide basic information—or their children could pay the ultimate price.

LESSONS FROM PEERS

What sort of things do kids learn from their peers? Listen to Kimberly, a twenty-one-year-old mother with eight- and two-year-old children: "When you are in the middle school and you run into a boy who's nineteen and cute, he can teach you about sex in a few minutes. You don't want him to be the one who teaches your kids about sex, but if you don't, he will."[1]

"Well of course I don't want my child to depend on his peers for sex information," some parents will say. "But the school will teach them what they need to know." If you sincerely believe that, you would be wise to carefully consider the kind of information that is being disseminated in the classrooms of our country. CSE, or Contemporary Sex Education, is now mandatory in sixteen states and the District of Columbia and is recommended by the state legislatures or boards of education of thirty others. Proponents of CSE claim that the courses are completely "value neutral," but that very phrase is an oxymoron. Nothing is value neutral. A value implies judgment. *Someone's* values are being communicated in every "value neutral" proposition, and if you hold to basic, Judeo-Christian ethics, you can be reasonably sure that the values taught are not your own.

Contemporary sex education instructors are coached to be non-judgmental in their teaching. Although they are advised to share their personal experiences, teachers are not to impose their opinions, even when it comes to the most important questions, such as, "What is the right time for me to begin having sex?" The teacher in this instance is encouraged to turn the question back to his or her students, asking, "How would *you* begin making that decision?"

Two leading sex educators recently spoke of their "high" hopes for sex education in the future in the widely read *Journal of Sex Education and Therapy*. Their words were sobering. They expressed the hope that sex education would knock down "the negative barriers that have been used to limit the number of sexual contacts" students might have, and that teenagers could be "rendered temporarily infertile through skin implants" of contraceptives so that they would be "free to engage in sexual activity without those fears that so inhibited their parents and grandparents."[2]

Given the liberal agenda of creators of curricula like these, what kinds of things might our children be learning in public school sex education courses? Here are a few sample statements taken from another children's sex education course called "Learning About Family Life":

Grownups sometimes forget to tell children that touching can also give people pleasure, especially when someone you love touches you. You can give yourself pleasure, too, and that's okay. When you touch your own genitals, it's called masturbating.

You are not just being sexual by having intercourse. You are being sexual when you throw your arms around your grandpa and give him a big hug.

When you are older, you can decide if you want to have sex. Most people do, because they like it and it's a very important way of showing that you love someone.[3]

But what kind of sex? Homosexual? Heterosexual? What about marriage? Doesn't it matter? Is "liking it" reason enough to partici-pate in a life-altering, soul-uniting act that God says is meant exclu-sively for marriage? Should I be like "most people"? Is there some-thing wrong if I am not?

Can you imagine how confusing such vague, amoral teaching is to children? In their efforts to be value neutral, the writers of this material have rendered it value-less. Nothing whatsoever is said about the context of sex. Little or nothing is said about the emo-tional and spiritual aspects of it, or of right and wrong.

How, then, can we as parents counter what our kids are being taught in classrooms and learning from their peers? The answer is simple: *by teaching them ourselves.* Parents were meant to be their children's teachers—regardless of the subject. That much is biblical: "O Israel, listen: Jehovah is our God, Jehovah alone. You must love him with all your heart, soul, and might. And you must think con-stantly about these commandments I am giving you today. You must teach them to your children and talk about them when you are at home or out for a walk; at bedtime and the first thing in the morning. Tie them on your finger, wear them on your forehead, and write them on the doorposts of your house!" (Deuteronomy 6:4–9, TLB).

Parents must arm themselves with sound information and solid, biblical principles...then get ready. Teaching children about sex is more than just preparing and delivering "the talk" at some arbitrary, preadolescent age. It involves diligent, consistent teaching through-out all stages of their physical, emotional, and spiritual develop-ment.

But if you are a parent, no one is more qualified than you to teach your children about their sexuality. Not the public school system, not the neighbor's kids, and not even the church! There are plenty of excellent resources available to prepare you for the task. I recommend these that I have found helpful: James Dobson's *Preparing for Adolescence,* Stan and Brenna Jones's series called *How and When to Talk to Your Children about Sex,* and Josh McDowell's *How to Help Your Child Say No.* Your local bookstore can order these for you.

HOW DO I BEGIN?

1. Know Your Goal

Whether you are the parent of a preschooler or a teenager, you must know your goal. What are you aiming for? Proverbs 7:1–4 says we are to aim for wisdom: "Follow my advice, my son; always keep it in mind and stick to it. Obey me and live! Guard my words as your most precious possession. Write them down, and also keep them deep within your heart. Love wisdom like a sweetheart; make her a beloved member of your family" (TLB).

We are to impart to our children not just information, but a body of knowledge, or a "world-view"—and sex illustrates clearly the difference in world-views. One with a Judeo-Christian world-view would likely practice sex exclusively within marriage. One with a non-Judeo-Christian world-view would be more likely to express sexual appetites apart from marriage. Observe how this is played out in today's culture: The debates over homosexuality, abortion, euthanasia, etc., can be understood by looking at opposing world-views. We need a world-view that establishes absolutes, from which valid conclusions can be drawn and wise decisions can be made.

On a flight to Israel my wife and I met Howard Metzenbaum, the retired United States senator from Ohio. When I recognized him, I introduced myself and we began to visit. During the eight-hour flight, I had the opportunity to ask him questions about

Watergate, particular pieces of legislation, the operation of the House and Senate, and the state of politics in general.

During the course of the conversation, Senator Metzenbaum described himself several times as a liberal, referring often to his liberal views. At some point, I mustered up the courage to ask him for clarification. "Senator," I said, "you have used the word 'liberal' in describing yourself and the things you have done. I'd like to ask you to define your use of that particular word, if you don't mind."

"Ed," he said, "I'd be happy to. A liberal is someone who believes in the Constitution of the United States of America and all of its amendments. He believes that every person in this land has equal rights and equal opportunity under the law, regardless of race, or creed, or national origin."

"I understand, Senator," I replied. "But I think it's interesting that while I would classify *myself* as a conservative, I believe in every single thing that you have just said. How can that be?"

He thought a minute, then answered, "Ed, it's because you are open-minded and understand the affairs of the world."

"Oh, no sir," I replied. "The truth is, I am very closed-minded about many things. In fact, people who know me would laugh at the idea that I'm an open-minded individual." Then I went on, "Senator, let me propose to you that the difference between a liberal and a conservative lies in his basic world-view. For example, let me ask you a question: Do you believe that Genesis 1:1 is literally true—that 'in the beginning God created the heavens and the earth'"?

He hesitated a moment, then scratched his head. "You know," he said, "they just found a 7,000-year-old man."

"I heard about that," I said.

"And there are a lot of linguistic problems in the Hebrew translation of the Old Testament."

I said, "Yes, Senator. I'm aware of some of those."

He waited a long time, then looked at me with piercing eyes and said, "No. I really don't believe that that is literally true."

"Senator," I said, "you're a liberal."

He smiled and nodded. And I suggested that perhaps this was a pretty good test to give anyone to begin to define his or her world-view.

What are the basics of a Christian world-view? First, that there is a God. Second, that God created this world in which we live. Third, that every person in this world is created and loved by God with a unique purpose and plan in mind. Finally, that it is possible for every individual to know God and His plan through His only Son, Jesus Christ. The choice rests with each individual. A perspective like this gives young people a sense of excitement about who they are, a sense of expectation about their future, a sense of reliance on God for direction and purpose, and a sense of responsibility for their personal choices.

Make it your primary goal to pass on to your children godly wisdom and a world-view that fosters true understanding. Remember—in the long run it is more important to instill our children with wisdom than to inundate them with facts. True wisdom will be to them like an intimate and lifelong friend: redeeming and life giving.

2. Start Early and Keep at It

The *shemah,* the passage from the Old Testament that instructed God's people on how to teach their children His ways (Deuteronomy 6:4–9), says that we are to teach both diligently and continually. In other words, it's not a one-shot deal. We are to seize every opportunity for teaching our children about sex, even as we do about all of life. When do you teach your children? When they get up in the morning. When they have breakfast. When you walk together. And how do you teach them? By signs. By Scripture. By ideas. By precepts.

Reducing instruction about sex into an infomercial delivered at some magic, preadolescent age is virtually worthless. Giving a one-time only "sex talk" to your child will have about as much impact as a coach giving a locker room pep talk to a team that has not learned the basics of the game. How do athletes learn to execute correctly when it's game time? By learning the fundamentals, by doing the drills that reinforce them, and by spending hour upon hour at practice. You teach your children about sexuality and its relationship to the whole of life by "layering" lesson upon lesson and conversation upon conversation until an ongoing dialogue is established. This takes discipline on the part of a parent! And it means we must "put aside our defenses and discomfort, work through our hesitancies, and risk not having the perfect answer or being shown to not know everything. Our children are worth it."[4]

3. Model What You Teach

Sex is one area of life where a "do as I say, not as I do" attitude on the part of parents is especially dangerous. Moms, Dads—your teaching and advice to your children about sexual standards is only as good as your own compliance. You cannot expect them to mirror an integrity that they have never seen modeled. Now, that does not mean that parents never make mistakes, but when they do, they should own up to them and simply say, "I was wrong."

I strongly believe that the best sex education any child ever receives is to have a mother and dad who love each other completely, exclusively, and devotedly. Nothing builds a stronger foundation for healthy sexuality in a child's life than to know that his or her parents are hopelessly, helplessly in love. Allow your children to see gestures of affection between the two of you. Communicate to them that you have a personal and private intimacy that goes beyond what they see—and that it is pleasing and good.

You and I have to do it right if we expect our children to choose rightly. The *shemah* says that we should love God with all our heart and soul and might—and that His commandments should be in *our* hearts so that we may teach them to our children. You cannot give away that which you do not have. A message of purity means nothing coming from a parent who is practicing immorality and lacks self-control.

4. Tell It Like It Is

Tell the truth—always. Let your children know the pressures they will face in our sexually charged world. Meet them where they are developmentally, and be honest with them about what other people do. Solomon's instructions to his sons in this area (see Proverbs 7) were straightforward; he pulled no punches. He told them what kind of women were out in the world. The truth is, most people don't hold a high view of sex or keep it exclusively for marriage. Your children need to understand that those who do will be considered a little strange. Sexual immorality and perversions exist. Temptation is real and is certainly nothing new, as this warning from Solomon illustrates: "I was looking out the window of my house one day, and saw a simple-minded lad, a young man lacking common sense, walking at twilight down the street to the house of this wayward girl, a prostitute. She approached him, saucy and pert, and dressed seductively. She was the brash, coarse type, seen often in the streets and markets, soliciting at every corner for men to be her lovers" (Proverbs 7:6–12, TLB).

Your children *will* face temptation. Solomon's children did. I did. My children did. There will be choices to make and always those who would tempt them to choose unwisely: " 'My bed is spread with lovely, colored sheets of finest linen imported from Egypt, perfumed with myrrh, aloes and cinnamon. Come on, let's take our fill of love until morning, for my husband is away on a long trip.'... So she seduced him with her pretty speech, her coaxing and her wheedling, until he yielded to her. He couldn't resist her flattery. He followed her as an ox going to the butcher, or as a stag that is trapped, waiting to be killed with an arrow through its heart. He was as a bird flying into a snare, not knowing the fate awaiting it there" (Proverbs 7:16–23, TLB).

Your children cannot be kept sheltered from the reality of the world in which they live. Tell them what they can expect. Tell it like it is. This is not optional. Temptations are real—but they can be overcome. So tell it like it is, and then...

5. Tell It Like It Ought to Be

Our world seems to think that knowledge about sex, about physiology, about contraception, etc., will enable children to make right decisions about sex. This simply is not true. If it were, statistics for abortion, AIDS, and illegitimate births would be declining dramatically. Knowing how to use a condom is not going to save this generation (or the next one) from disease, death, or disastrous relationships. "Safe sex" is not sex with a condom. Safe sex is exclusive, faithful, committed sex between one man and one woman for life. Anything else carries with it the explosive potential to destroy lives—physically, emotionally, and every other way. Parents need to continually paint a picture of what God meant sex to be: good, right, pure, and exciting, within a lifetime commitment of marriage.

The world will not deliver this message to our children. Who will they hear it from if not from us? It is a time to sound the alarm, raise the volume, and address the deadly misdirection of a generation raised on sexual myth, media hype, and misunderstanding. Instead, we need the sexual clarity that comes from the Creator of sex, Who alone is able to fill all of our relationships with purpose, power, and passion.

What to Teach...and When

When do parents begin to teach their children about sex? Ideally, when the child is born. From birth to age five, we can start laying the groundwork for a lifetime of positive teaching about sexuality.

1. Ages 0–5: Laying the Groundwork

Very early on, parents can do some simple things that will make sexual education less daunting and intimidating for parent and child.

First, begin to use correct terminology for all body parts, including the genitals. When a parent calls an arm an arm, and a leg a leg, but uses euphemisms to label the genitals, they are unknowingly sending the wrong message. Call a penis a penis. Call a vagina a vagina. Don't make up words because you find the real ones uncomfortable to say. Your child learns thousands of words from birth to age five. Unless you make a big deal out of the ones that deal with sexual anatomy, they will accept them just as readily as any other word.

Second, during this time it is important that children learn it is OK to ask Mom and Dad questions about anything, including their bodies and the mechanics of physical life. They need to know, generally speaking, where babies come from and how they "get in and out." We tried to do this in our family, but I confess it wasn't always easy.

When our oldest son, Ed, was in prekindergarten, a great teaching opportunity presented itself. His school teacher became pregnant. Ed would come home every afternoon reporting that his teacher was "getting bigger and bigger," and he was concerned that something might be wrong with Mrs. Rogers. As I recall, Jo Beth just told him that sometimes moms gain a little weight, but that she was sure Mrs. Rogers would be just fine.

As the weeks went by, Ed's concern grew. Jo Beth talked to me about it, and I finally told her that if he asked again, *she* would have to tell him something! That's called passing the buck, by the way, and I am not proud of it. The next time he asked, Jo Beth carefully explained that Mrs. Rogers was going to have a baby, that the baby was inside of her growing, and it would come out at just the right time.

In perfect, four-year-old logic, Ed asked if the baby had a blanket in there too. Jo Beth said no, that it was kept warm by its mother's body and that it had plenty of food to eat as well. Ed thought a little bit longer, then looked at his mother and asked, "Did I grow in you like that?"

"Yes, son," she answered, "you sure did."

Ed looked her square in the eye and said with utter conviction, "I don't believe it." End of conversation.

When another one of my sons was born, my wife's sister was there with one of her daughters, who was also about four at the time. She had been brought up in a family of girls and had never seen a naked baby boy. When it was time to change the baby's diaper, she was amazed to see that little boys and little girls have different equipment.

"What's that?" she asked.

My sister-in-law patiently explained the difference between boys and girls, noting that little boys have physical attributes that little girls do not. Her daughter took all this information in, then looked at her mother and her aunt and said cheerfully, "Well, it's kind of cute, isn't it?"

This is the age to nurture the development of a child's self-esteem and to interpret physical facts in terms of God's creative purpose, i.e., "That's your (name of body part)—God made it, and it is good." Reinforce the concept of family as the primary place to experience love, lifelong devotion, unity, and safety. It is important that we convey to our children a sense of openness and honesty about the way we are made and that we answer their simple questions simply, gladly, and directly. The way we handle these teachable moments is very, very important, and it is never too early to begin.

2. Ages 6–9: Branching Out

From age six to nine, children should come to understand the basic facts of intercourse and reproduction. Provide as much accurate information as your child is ready to understand. Look for opportunities to offer information about sex, even when you are not asked. Teach your child to develop a vocabulary to describe these functions, as well as their own body parts and those of the opposite sex. By now they are hearing this from their friends, from teachers and/or textbooks, and from television, so it is important that they hear it from you, too, to get the facts straight.

As much as possible, focus your explanations on human beings, not animals. Nonhuman, "birds and bees" analogies can confuse a child and can subtly depersonalize sex and separate it from loving commitment. Determine what your children already know and clear up any misinformation they may have as a result of others' (or your own!) teaching. Let your word be the one they can count on to be true and informed, over any other. Don't be afraid of their knowledge or inquisitiveness. Remember—sex is a gift from God and a good and positive part of life.

3. Ages 10–13: Growing Up

This is the time to begin going into more detail about intercourse and to explain the changes that take place in boys and girls during adolescence. Praise your kids for asking questions and for demonstrating a comprehension of what they have been taught so far. Children of this age should understand how conception takes place and what abortion is. They need to know especially about the general stages of their own growth and about their ensuing emotional and physical development, including facts about menstruation, wet dreams, and masturbation.

It is also a good idea to treat the issue of sexual abuse here, making them aware that there are those who would take advantage of their emerging sexuality. I wish this were not necessary, but it is. With the development of computer technology and the growth of the information superhighway, pedophiles and others who would prey on children can even lurk on your home computer!

Remember that none of this information should be disseminated in a vacuum. From birth through the time your children leave home, it is imperative that you use every opportunity available to put sexuality into a framework of God's moral law and His perfect plan for its expression. Every time a parent gives a child a piece of information or an explanation, he or she should ask the question, "So what?"—and answer it. It is absolutely inexcusable for parents to allow children to fumble around for answers with regard to their sexuality, or to be left to "figure it all out on their own." We need to let our children know we have been where they are, and that we can help them know what to expect and how to deal with it.

Parents who need incentive to deal openly, candidly, and freely with their children where sex is concerned need only to recall their own adolescence. Remember the confusion, the shame, the curiosity, the fear that you went through during those years? Do you want your children's experience to be more positive? More informed? Do you want them to understand the deep, deep truth that sex is a beautiful gift from God and must be handled with great care and respect? That they are "fearfully and wonderfully made" and that God has a plan for their lives? Then you must tell them. No one else will—or certainly no one who loves them more.

4. Ages 14–18: Taking Flight

During the high school years, you will determine the appropriate age for your child to begin to date and establish guidelines for dating. This is the time to talk frankly about kissing, petting, date rape, and the very real physical, spiritual, and emotional consequences of sexual experimentation. Many teens today are actually making pledges to remain sexually pure until their wedding day (and their parents are pledging to prayerfully support their abstinence) through programs like "True Love Waits" and others. This can be a great source of encouragement and strength to young people and their parents!

Despite what many have been led to believe, teenage abstinence *is* a viable option. Teenagers do not *have* to have sex. It is not a required rite of passage to adulthood. Contrary to popular belief, everyone is *not* doing it. It is difficult to abstain, certainly. But it is entirely possible.

What do teens who choose to reserve sex for marriage have in common? I believe three things.

First, they have a sense of themselves as special individuals with a unique contribution to make to the world in which we live. Someone—a parent, a teacher, a grandparent, a friend—has made these young people feel valuable. They are secure in the knowledge that they are loved, because that love has been demonstrated by significant others. They have learned to see themselves as God sees them: precious and infinitely valuable.

Second, teenagers who are able to wait for sex have a reverence for God and His principles. They are not afraid to refuse something they know is wrong, usually because someone taught them right from wrong at an early age. They have refused to buy into situational ethics or "movable" morality. They have fixed standards. They believe in absolute truth.

Finally, teenagers who are able to wait prize the worth of others. A recent college graduate put it this way: "If I really loved someone, why would I run the risk of hurting them just so I could be temporarily gratified? Why would I not want to protect them in the same way God wants to protect me? If I really loved this other person, then I would want what is best for them in the long run." Those who are committed to purity do not use others for their own pleasure. They respect the needs and feelings of others and consider those needs as equal in importance to their own.

The teenage years are the years in which everything you have taught them will be put to the test. The time between adolescence and adulthood is so brief, but so very, very important. In just a few short years, your children will leave the protected nest of your home and go out into the world alone for the first time. Have you prepared them to discern right from wrong and to avoid the trap of sexual promiscuity? Have you established the kind of relationship with your teenager that will keep the lines of communication open, even if the news is not good? If you work at anything, work at this. To consistently respond to your children with unconditional love sends a clear signal that yours will always be a "safehouse" for communication.

PUTTING IT ALL TOGETHER

How do you teach your children about sex? You start with a goal in mind. You begin early and keep at it. You model what you teach. Then you tell it like it is and like it ought to be. You instruct in ways that are appropriate to a child's development and current level of understanding.

Does this sound tough? It is! If it were easy, everyone would be doing an A+ job! While I believe parents have the primary responsibility for teaching their children about sex, others can certainly contribute to the process, including teachers, relatives, and friends. But Mom or Dad—the buck stops with you. The important thing is not to abdicate your parental responsibility out of fear, discomfort, or ignorance.

If your child is taking sex education at school, find out what the class is teaching. Don't just breathe a sigh of relief and consider the issue taken care of. Know what kinds of facts and values are being communicated, and strive to place that information within the context of the world-view you are trying to impart to your children.

Realize, however, that "because I say so," or even, "because God says so," will not always be reason enough for your kids to adopt your point of view. Such close-ended arguments might even undermine your cause. What your children need to understand is that God's way works. It is good for them—no, it is best. "Traditional

Christian sexual morality does make exquisite sense. It is, like all of God's wisdom, a thing of beauty and grace. God's Law is a path that guides us toward wholeness; it is a lamp that shows the way through the darkest night."[5]

What parent doesn't want wholeness for his children? Don't you? Then be ready to give a reasonable defense for God's guidelines of sexual expression. Teach your children to follow His commandments in this, as in every area of life. You can be sure that blessing will follow obedience and that His statutes are for our survival, our good, and our good pleasure.

PART TWO

Refusing Cheap Substitutes

CHAPTER SEVEN

"But We Love Each Other!"

Sex and the Single Person

In a dimly lit café, an attractive single woman runs down her list of previous lovers to a single man who is infatuated with her. (The two slept together once after meeting at the wedding of mutual friends, but she is presently engaged to another man.) He listens slack-jawed as she recounts her sexual experience with no less than thirty-three former lovers one by one—commenting flippantly on some aspect of their sexual technique. When she is done (his is the next-to-the-last name on her list), the man is still smitten with her, and his only embarrassment is over his own relative lack of sexual experience, having had just six or seven partners!

You would have to have your head buried deeply in the sand to imagine that unmarried people are not having sexual intercourse. While this scene is from a highly popular movie and not from real life, statistics reveal at least the young man's experience to be about average. The previously cited University of Chicago study shows that 58 percent of the male population surveyed reported having had from zero to five sexual partners since age eighteen. By contrast, only 3 percent of the females surveyed reported having had more than twenty-one sexual partners, making the well-experienced young woman in this film a member of a very small minority.[1]

The undeniable truth is, many men and women today are having sex at younger and younger ages, with an increasing number of partners. And although 90 percent of Americans have married by the time they are thirty, the same men and women who are becoming sexually active *earlier* are also marrying *later.* The obvious result? More and more sexually active singles.

WHAT'S A PIECE OF PAPER, ANYWAY?

Admittedly, the vast majority of adults today are having sex—whether they are married or not. Marriage is simply no longer recognized as the accepted "home" for sexual intimacy. In the late 1950s, when unmarried actress Ingrid Bergman became pregnant with the child of director Roberto Rosselini, a scandal ensued. Her career was seriously damaged, and her personal reputation suffered—although she later married Rosselini, and the two had another child together.

Today the Bergman/Rosselini affair would not make a ripple in the scandal pond. Politicians openly admit marital infidelity but insist it is no reflection on their character. Three million opposite-sex couples currently live together as "unmarried partners with a close personal relationship," in Census Bureau language. "Cohabitation," says one prominent sociologist, "is the standard; it is no longer a deviant relationship at all."[2] Our society's increasing nonchalance about premarital sex signals an alarming erosion of the sacredness of marriage.

Single adults who are *not* sexually active are subject to more ridicule and misunderstanding than those who move from partner to partner with little or no thought of permanent commitment. Society's standards have changed. When "love" is a part of any relationship, sexual intimacy is not just accepted, it is assumed. To love without having sexual intercourse is considered repressive and a denial of personal rights. Philip Turner, dean of Berkeley Divinity School at Yale University, writes that we have so fused the ideas of sexuality, self, and identity that it is "easy to understand why more and more people believe it is wrong to deny a sexual relation to oneself or to anyone else simply on the basis of marital status, sexual orientation, or gender identification."[3] In other words, sex has become a social entitlement whose chief prerequisite is anything that goes by the name of love.

But what *kind* of love are we talking about? The love that makes sexual involvement acceptable for the majority is not great love, not sacrificial love, not transcendent love. It is not the incredible, Christ-like love described by the apostle Paul in his letter to the Corinthians. It is rather a weak, watered-down version of the real thing. "True love," philosopher Peter Kreeft insists, "includes awe. This is one of the great secrets of sex and marriage that our age has tragically forgotten: awe at the mystery that sex is. No true mystery is ever explained away. Sex, death, love, evil, beauty, life, the soul, God—these remain forever infinite mysteries that we never exhaust and should not want to. They are like the ocean, for us to swim in, not like a glass of water for us to drink and drain dry."[4]

Much of what goes by the name of love today is really either convenience, codependence, or lust. It is love in name only. "Intimacy" is another word often substituted nowadays for love—and apparently if intimacy is the goal, any kind of behavior is admissible. We no longer speak of husbands and of wives. Instead, we refer to our current "partner," meaning the person we are having sex with at the present time.

I was stung by this truth as I flipped through the pages of several mainstream women's publications, filled with articles about love-making with your "partner," communicating with your "partner," handling conflict with your "partner." It seems odd to spend so much time and effort analyzing and improving a relationship with a partner who refuses to make a commitment. Apparently "partners" who offer no promise of permanence still require a tremendous amount of attention and emotional energy!

In this freewheeling climate, the church's traditional teaching—that sexual intercourse is not for the unmarried—is seen as harsh, unjust, and completely out-of-date. "But we love each other!" has become the insistent cry of the majority. Parents and educators, certain that adolescent children will not be able to resist their natural sexual urges, are throwing in the towel and pitching in for condoms. High school and college students, certain that "everyone is doing it," are sleeping with multiple partners and coming to marriage (if and when they marry) with tremendous emotional baggage. And once-married adults who are divorced or widowed are rationalizing that since they've been married before, they couldn't possibly be expected to abstain from having sex simply because they no longer have a husband or a wife.

THREE KINDS OF UNCOMMITTED SEX

If the majority of unmarried adults are having sex, what kind of sex is it? Simply put, it is *uncommitted sex*. This is always true, no matter what the participants claim. Sex outside of marriage is uncommitted sex, period. It can be nothing else. You can dress it up, clean it up, shine it up, and give it a nice-sounding name, but you cannot change its very nature.

I cannot count the number of times I have heard unmarried couples who are ready to have sex but not to marry claim "we are married in our hearts and in the eyes of God." Justifying further they issue a challenge: "What difference does a little piece of paper make?" The difference the piece of paper makes is enormous: It is the difference between *intent* and *action*.

Nowhere else in life do we expect a contract to be acknowledged without active commitment. Nowhere else do we insist that "intent" equals "action." It is not possible to put a contract on a house you *intend* to buy and take up residence without a mortgage commitment. It is impossible to talk a car dealer into letting you test drive a car for a month or two before you actually make a payment. No financial institution will loan money you *intend* to pay back without obtaining your signature on loan papers—and many times not even then without securing collateral.

All of these desires might reflect good intentions, but deals are not consummated on good intentions. Commitment in the form of action is always required. No action equals no commitment. Those who are sexually active apart from true, lifelong commitment are simply saying "so what?" "who knows?" or "oh, well…" and placing their lives and their futures at risk.

"So What?" Sex

A lot of singles are having the kind of sex that I call "So what?" sex. It's strictly recreational. Two individuals come together to meet their immediate physical or emotional needs, and nothing more. No commitment is implied or expected, even though the participants may claim to be in love or to have feelings for one another. The problem with "So what?" sex is that it makes too little of us and of our sexuality. In fact, it cheapens our real value, worth, and dignity. God claims that we were created a little lower than the angels, not a little higher than the animals. "So what?" sex is lowest-common-denominator stuff, and whatever satisfaction it brings is shallow and fleeting, at best.

"Who Knows?" Sex

In addition to "So what?" sex, many singles participate in what I call "Who knows?" sex. "Who knows?" sex is experimental. Again, there is no commitment, but there is at least an interest in commitment—either expressed or unexpressed. These individuals may be looking for long-term love (and even considering one another as candidates), but they are not yet willing to commit. "Who knows?" sex might lead to commitment, but most participants find themselves involved in a series of "Who knows?" affairs that never seem to lead to anything permanent.

"Oh, Well..." Sex

Finally, there is "Oh, well..." sex, or what some call preceremonial sex. "Oh, well..." sex involves two people who are in an exclusive relationship and either say they plan to marry at some point in the future or are actually engaged to be married. They may even vow to abstain from sexual intercourse until they become husband and wife but get carried away before the ceremony. Many Christian couples find themselves involved in "Oh, well..." sexual relationships with their eventual mate. Their attitude seems to be, "Oh, well...we didn't intend for it to happen, but we're getting married anyway."

WHAT'S WRONG WITH UNCOMMITTED SEX?

The problem with uncommitted sex is that in every instance, uncommitted sex is a second-rate sexual experience. Whether an unmarried couple is involved in "So what?" sex, "Who knows?" sex, or "Oh, well…" sex, they are outside of God's plan, because He designed sex for the total-life commitment of marriage. Call it old-fashioned, call it Victorian, or call it closed-minded, but it is true. It is God's way and not simply an unfounded belief.

Biblical sexual morality—the truth that sex is sacred and holy and is intended only for husband and wife—is based on two absolutes: who we are and what sex is. In his excellent book *Making Choices*, Peter Kreeft writes that "the rules of sexual morality, like all real morality, are not an invention of men but of God, not artificial rules of a game society decided to play, but natural rules of a spiritual organism, based on the inherent, built-in design and purpose of human nature. It is not the changeable rules of a game we designed, but the unchangeable rules of the operating manual written by the Designer of our human nature."[5]

No matter what the standards of our society may be, we can change neither the very nature of sex or our own human nature. Sexual intercourse is a life-altering, physical, spiritual, mental, and emotional experience with great and powerful ramifications. "The most casual of sexual liaisons may be like some great submarine earthquake, sending its slow and unfathomable shock waves not only into every corner of the lives of the lovers themselves, but throughout the entire nexus of family and friends, extending even to the unborn and to whole future generations."[6] Sex is never insignificant, never casual. It matters, and it matters deeply.

And what about us? We are made for wholeness. Our sexuality is woven into our very being and was never intended to be parceled out apart from our heart, our spirit, our mind, and our will. Men and women are fearfully and wonderfully created in the image of God, and every one of us has been deeply loved by Him and designed for relationship with Him (Psalm 139:13–18). There is more to us than just our physical bodies and the span of our earthly years. We are eternal, precious, and complex—and sex is a part of that complexity, but it is by no means the whole.

Three Warnings from the Designer

Warnings are a familiar part of our everyday lives. A quick trip around the house from kitchen to bedroom to bathroom will uncover a host of them. Your hairdryer probably has a tag attached that recommends you not use the appliance while bathing. Household cleaning products display warnings against everything from fumes to prolonged skin contact. Prescription drugs often bear warning labels about recommended dosages and possible side effects. Even a seemingly harmless packet of scented potpourri carries the warning that it should not be ingested!

Are any of these things inherently bad or harmful when they are rightly used? No. But in some cases, their misuse could be damaging, even deadly. So it is with sex. It is not inherently bad. In fact, just the opposite is true. It is a good gift, a fantastic gift, created and given to us by a loving God. It was not designed by Him to be harmful in any way. But wrongly used, it can be incredibly destructive—physically, emotionally, and spiritually.

God, the designer of sex, warns us of three particular areas of sexual prohibition. First, there must be no adultery. Nothing arbitrary there. Sex with someone who is already married is prohibited. Second, there must be no fornication, or sex between unmarried persons. This statement is made five times in the New Testament and is implied another twenty-three times. Finally, there is to be no *pornea,* or lustful, provocative activity between unmarried adults (see 1 Corinthians 6:9–11).

God's prohibitions against these specific activities are warnings against wrong use from the Designer of our sexuality. They are for our protection and our good. Like all warnings, if we choose to ignore them, we do so at our own risk. While many warnings today are issued to protect the manufacturer against the end user, God's warnings are not. Instead, they protect the user from his or her own misuse. They are made not for the manufacturer's protection—God needs no protection. They are made for our good alone.

THE PRICE OF UNCOMMITTED SEX

It would be easy to begin with statistics that illustrate the high price of uncommitted sex, but they've been reeled off so frequently that we have become almost numb to their impact. Everyone by now has heard the numbers of unwanted pregnancies, abortions, sexually transmitted diseases, and single-parent homes. Instead, consider this story, told by a young woman who violated God's second warning and learned the hard way that sexual promiscuity could cost her in ways she never imagined.

We'll call her Carol. You might know someone like her. She grew up in the church and became a Christian at an early age. Today she works with teenagers and is involved in ministry to single adults. She is cute and bubbly and full of life. She has been celibate for several years and carries within her body a sexually-transmitted disease that will be with her for life.

> My parents told me as a young person that they hoped I would not have sex before I was married, but to use protection if I did. Since they didn't take a direct, hard stand for purity—neither did I. The minister in my church said, "No sex before marriage," but he never said why. So when the boys in high school started putting on the pressure, I gave in. I had sex with my high school boyfriends and later with my college boyfriends. It wasn't so much the sex for me, I just wanted to feel loved and accepted. Deep in my heart, I knew God did not approve—but I tried not to think about that.
>
> By my senior year in college, I was beginning to see that none of these sexual relationships really gave me what I was looking for. I was tired of giving myself totally to a guy, then having my heart broken when it ended. It happened over and over again. I remember one Sunday afternoon I was having lunch with several friends from my sorority— all of whom had gone out and partied the night before. All of them were sleeping with their boyfriends. The thought suddenly occurred to me that I wasn't like them. This was

not who I really was. I was different. I had to be. I knew that there had to be more to life than partying and cheap sex.

I was ready to change. I started attending church again. I felt guilty for my actions, but I still didn't understand why God said "no sex outside of marriage." I resolved to stop having sex with my boyfriend of three months. I told him, "No more—that's it," and he said, "Just one more time." I didn't want to have sex with him again, but I did. It was hard to say no, and I still wanted his love. He used a condom, but it didn't matter. I woke up the next morning with a virus called herpes. Even when it is not apparent, it is dormant in my body. It will never leave.

Four months later, I graduated from college. I moved to a new city and found a church. I rededicated my life to Christ and began to find in my relationship with Him the unconditional love I had searched for in all the wrong places. I made a decision to remain celibate until I marry—one that I have kept for over four years. It took time, but I learned to forgive myself and to forgive the men who used me sexually.

I've had dating relationships since that time that were fulfilling and healthy—and not about sex. I've kept my promise to abstain. Recently I was in a relationship with a great guy that became serious. When we began talking about marriage, I felt I had to tell him about my disease, but when I did, he couldn't bring himself to make a commitment to me. It broke my heart and brought back every bad thing that I had thought about myself—but I survived and today I am stronger for the experience.

I still struggle with the reality of living with a sexually transmitted disease and of one day having to face the issue again with someone that I love. But I've learned that Christ's love is sufficient and abounding, more than enough for every situation. What I have with Him is more than any guy could ever give me. His constant grace keeps me hopeful that I will one day have a fulfilling marriage that's about love and acceptance and not just about sex.

Carol's experience perfectly illustrates both the physical and emotional price many pay when involved with uncommitted sex. She became one of the twelve million teenagers and adults *each year* who contracts a sexually transmitted disease. And while no one ever explained to her why she should reserve sex for marriage, she came to understand why in her own heart and life. It was hurtful. And it wasn't nearly satisfying enough.

While Carol's disease was not life-threatening, others who have gambled with premarital sex have lost everything. Thirty-five-year-old LaGena Lookabill Greene, a former North Carolina Junior Miss, is infected with AIDS. She has seen her white cell count plummet from a near-normal 965 to 14, and she has already picked out her casket and planned her memorial service. In 1986, Greene had sex with NASCAR race driver Tim Richmond, who she believes knew he was HIV-positive at the time. He is now dead.

Richmond was a good-looking, free-spirited man who lived the fast life. His womanizing shocked even the journalists who covered the racing beat. "I walked in on Tim at a big public party, and he was having sex with a woman on a counter," one longtime racing writer recalls.[7] Richmond pursued Greene for six years and proposed marriage to her three times. Until he came along, she had had only one boyfriend, whom she dated from age twelve through her junior year at the University of North Carolina.

Greene contracted AIDS from Tim Richmond on September 10, 1986, in a New York City hotel. He asked her to fly to New York with him for dinner, booked a hotel suite, filled it with roses, and proposed to her a final time, promising to be a devoted husband and father. LaGena accepted this time, and they consummated their relationship.

"I believed that by giving myself to Tim physically our union marked the beginning of a lifetime of mutual commitment," she said. "We never made love again. Now I see that day as the end of my life as I had known it."[8] He did not call her again for two years and four months, and she learned of his AIDS diagnosis not from him, but from a sportswriter. When LaGena publicly announced her disease, she was contacted by thirty women in the Charlotte area alone who had had sex with Richmond and were also HIV-positive.

In what turned out to be their final conversation, LaGena told Tim, "I know you gave me this disease and that you knew you had AIDS when you asked me to marry you. But I forgive you."[9] She said that he never acknowledged the deception, but thanked her for her forgiveness.

And don't think it's just the promiscuous who suffer the consequences of uncommitted sex. Other lives are affected as well, because none of us is an island unto himself. Consider this story of another young woman who found it impossible to connect with a man she was dating because of the guilt he felt over his past relationships:

> I learned in a recent relationship that there is a downside to sexual promiscuity that some people don't realize. It's the danger of moving from one unhealthy extreme to the other…or from having no boundaries to establishing boundaries that are impossible to get past.
>
> I met a very committed Christian man and we began to date. He was serious about his beliefs and we had (or so I thought) similar outlooks on life. At first he really pursued me, but soon, whenever I would respond, he would back away. If we spent a lot of time together or shared anything on a deep level, he seemed to become more distant as a result.
>
> He was what I would call sporadically affectionate. If he hugged me or held my hand or kissed me, I could be pretty sure he would disappear for a few days afterward. We heard a sermon one Sunday in church together about abstinence and he told me emphatically that he was not a virgin. Since he was in his thirties, I certainly was not shocked. Then he asked me if I was a virgin and I told him yes. From that point on, our relationship seemed to slowly unravel.
>
> I didn't really understand what was happening until he

confessed one night that he had spent a period of several years in his twenties and early thirties being "repeatedly, willfully disobedient" in the sexual area. Without thinking, I asked him how many sexual partners he had had, and his response was "I don't know." Ten—or any number—would not have shocked me I guess, but "I don't know" just blew me away. How could you not know something like that?

Then I began to understand his on-again/off-again actions that had been so confusing. He apparently had never had an adult dating relationship that did not include sex. He was trying to abstain now, and the easiest way to do that was to keep an emotional and physical distance in place that precluded any kind of intimacy. He could not forgive himself for his sexual past and did not think he deserved someone without one. He told me he prayed I would find a better man and that God would give him what he deserved. I remember thinking the last thing any of us should want from God is what we deserve.

This man's past, even though God had forgiven it, kept him from having any kind of emotionally healthy relationship because he still felt guilty and vulnerable to the same old temptations. I don't expect to find many other adults who have waited into their thirties for sex, but I do pray for someone who loves God with a passion, understands and accepts His grace, and trusts Him enough to walk the very fine line between caution against sin and the hope of committed love. I didn't share this person's sexual past, but it hurt me just the same.

Physical consequences. Emotional consequences. These are the inevitable results of disregarding God's warnings about the expression of our sexuality. But also there are *spiritual* consequences. To see what those might be, we can consider the words of a man who strayed sexually, then found himself far from God as a result: "God! Please have pity on me. You are always merciful! Please wipe away my sins. Wash me clean from all of my sin and guilt. I know about my sins, and I cannot forget my terrible guilt. You are really the one I have sinned against; I have disobeyed you and have done wrong. Turn your eyes from my sin and cover my guilt. Create pure thoughts in me and make me faithful again. Don't chase me away from you, or take your Holy Spirit away from me" (Psalm 51:1–4, 9–11, CEV).

These desperate words were written by a king who had committed adultery. His name was David. He penned them after he was confronted by another man about what he thought was his secret sin. These words show that he suffered the spiritual consequences of his actions long before he was found out. He suffered separation from God and felt estranged from Him. Why? Because sin—any sin, sexual or otherwise—always separates us from God, and God's Word tells us that as long as we hide sin in our heart, God does not hear our prayers (Psalm 66:18).

The king's sin kept him awake at night, haunted his days, and weighed his heart down. It made him miserable and ashamed and became such a burden to him that his heart began to break. He was the leader of a nation and a man after God's own heart—but no one is bulletproof to the spiritual consequences of sexual sin, no matter how rich, how famous, how important he has become.

HOW CLOSE TO THE EDGE CAN I STAND?

Anytime God's parameters for sexual expression are taught, someone inevitably asks a question like this: "Well, if unmarried persons are not to have sexual intercourse, what *can* they do with one another and still be within bounds?" That's just like human nature, isn't it? We gravitate toward the far edge of every prohibition, wondering just how close to danger we can lurk without disaster. Teenagers especially want to know, "How far can we go and still be OK in God's eyes?"

The answer to that question (which is addressed specifically *nowhere* in Scripture, by the way) lies in God's third warning: the prohibition of *pornea,* or lustful activity between the unmarried. Bluntly speaking, any activity that is sexually provocative to the parties involved should be avoided. In other words, it is wrong for unmarried men and women to tease and stimulate one another sexually to the point of frustration, even stopping short of intercourse.

Anyone who has ever competed as an athlete understands how tough it is to prepare physically, mentally, and emotionally for the game...and not play. My son Ed went to Florida State on a basketball scholarship. Ed was a terrific high school player who played nearly every minute of every game, but as a freshman at Florida State, he spent a lot of time on the bench. He took the court before each game with the rest of the team, made his practice shots, ran through warmups, did stretching exercises, dribbling exercises, and free-throw drills. When the time for tipoff came, he would have worked up a light sweat. Then the starting lineups would be announced, and Ed—loose, warmed up, and ready to play—would take his seat at the end of the bench.

He was trained, prepared, and disciplined...but he didn't get into the game. It wasn't his time. But I can assure you that as a result, he was one frustrated young athlete. Everything in him was aching to play. Every instinct. Every emotion. Every muscle. He was so close to the action that he could taste it, but the actual game was just out of reach for him. I doubt the situation was something Ed would have chosen for himself, had the choice been his. He did not enjoy it.

If you are unmarried, the time for you to enjoy the expression of your sexuality through sexual intercourse has not yet arrived. It is not your time. Don't choose to make yourself miserable and frustrated by constantly "warming up" for a game you are not slated to play. It will not build you up. It may instead enslave you. Avoid the activities you know are certain to raise both your level of sexual excitement *and* your level of sexual frustration. God's advice is simply that we steer our lives as far as we can from sexual temptation: "Flee from youthful lusts, and pursue righteousness, faith, love and peace, with those who call on the Lord from a pure heart" (2 Timothy 2:22).

At the risk of sounding even older than I am, let me suggest how an unmarried man or woman might practically heed this word of instruction, using the stages of physical activity in a typical romantic relationship. What I would call *stage one* in physical expression is marked by kissing, hugging, and holding hands. These actions are not particularly passionate, but affectionate, although certain ways of kissing and embracing can, of course, be very arousing. I believe these stage one activities have a real place in a dating relationship, and from my experience, they can be a lot of fun in and of themselves. If you and your partner have this kind of affectionate feeling toward one another, I think these expressions are healthy and fine and good. That's stage one.

Stage two involves what I would call light petting. Light petting is sexual stimulation that does not have sexual intercourse as its goal. It crosses the line from affection to passion, although the couple remains clothed. Light petting builds sexual tension through fondling without relieving that tension through orgasm.

Stage three is heavy petting. Heavy petting involves stimulation of another person's sexually excitable areas, including the genitals, while unclothed. This contact can lead to orgasm, and often does.

In stage two and stage three, many couples who intend to go no further than petting will end up having intercourse. Why? Basically, there are two reasons. One, the further you go physically, the more focused you become on intercourse as the ultimate goal. In fact, light petting and heavy petting are the activities of foreplay, which, as its name suggests, is intimate physical "play" leading up to sexual intercourse. And second, there exists what can be called the "law of diminishing returns." What was exciting and stimulating the first time around is a little less so the next time. We hit a plateau of satiation which requires us to repeatedly raise our level of physical involvement to reach comparable levels of satisfaction. As a result, without a commitment to a standard, one can easily be enticed to go a step further…and further…and further.

One author has said that the only difference between petting and foreplay is intent—but when the emotional and physical passions become engaged as they are in petting, intent is easily confused or abandoned. That is why I believe stage two and stage three activities are inappropriate for a dating relationship: Their aim is not to express affection and appreciation, but to experience sexual excitement, something God intended for marriage partners only.

Writer Tim Stafford puts it this way: "When you go further...I think you generally stop speaking the language of love. Why? Because you have to stop somewhere short of intercourse. Some people can't—they lose control. Some people lose the desire to stop. Some people keep control, but they do so at the cost of feeling frustrated. Instead of feeling warm toward each other, they feel overheated. I have never known this to help a relationship to grow, especially when people spend hours together revving up their motors and pushing the brake at the same time."[10]

The key phrase there is "I have never known this [going further] to help a relationship to grow." That's because the impact felt by the presence of sex in an uncommitted relationship is huge. Couples who engage in sex when their relationship is new and commitment is absent (in the form of marriage) will soon learn that growth in other areas is easily stunted. Why? Because it's easier to have sex than to develop true intimacy. It is easier—for the moment at least—to pet than to talk deeply and truthfully. It is more exciting—for the moment at least—to have intercourse than to establish trust and security. As a result, many couples trade the growth of long-term intimacy for short-term physical pleasure, sabotaging any chance they may have at real knowledge and commitment.

This is a trade made even more tragic when we realize that the average married couple in America spends less than eighteen minutes each week making love. That is less than 2 percent of their time as man and wife devoted to the *physical* expression of their intimacy. Now don't misunderstand. I am not saying that sex is unimportant to a marriage! It is vitally important and essential for a marriage to be all that it should be. But I *am* saying that sex is not enough to build a marriage on.

I am amazed at single people who insist that they would never marry someone without sleeping together first to see if they are "sexually compatible." Listen, if you have developed companionate love, and affectionate love, and self-sacrificing love, and you are physically attracted to one another, you will almost certainly be "sexually compatible." But if you have failed to develop these other aspects of your relationship, the best sex life in the world is not going to carry you through a lifetime together. Good icing can't save a bad cake!

So what is the bottom line? Just this: The best choice for unmarried men and women is *pure sex*. That's right. For the single person, that means enjoying the expression of their God-given sexual nature in myriad ways, but saving the total, physical expression of sexual intercourse for the commitment of marriage. Some may ask, is that possible? The answer is an enthusiastic "yes!" Well, then—how is it done? I was hoping you'd ask. But first, let's look at another area of sexual temptation faced by many single adults.

CHAPTER EIGHT

Just Say Yes!

A Plan for Pure

Relational Intimacy

J ust say no" was a popular antidrug slogan that stuck. It was the rallying cry in a long campaign against teenage drug abuse, and the phrase still pops up frequently today. But whether the "no" is a response to illegal drugs, drinking to excess, premarital sex, or even the consumption of high-fat foods, saying "no" alone just isn't enough to effect lasting behavior change.

It's not that "no's" aren't valid. They are. It was not by mistake that most of the Ten Commandments were written by God in the negative. These immutable "Thou shalt not's" will remain in place for as long as this planet is in orbit (longer!), in spite of movie mogul Ted Turner's attempts to rewrite them into ten politically correct, user-friendly human initiatives.

There is nothing wrong with "no," but our culture has certainly begun to think that there might be. Many say this backlash against "no" can be traced to the college campus of the sixties, where students were taught a moral relativism that asked not, "Is it right?" but "Is it right for me, now, or does it feel good in this situation?" In an age of relativism, "no" is valid, but "no" is not enough. The emphatic "no" that offers no motivation but fear for doing what is right is nothing but a joyless exercise in legalism. And the plain truth is, where premarital sex is concerned, most stopped saying "no" years ago.

A *USA Today* article confirms that the majority of teens today have sex before age twenty. In the late 1950s, 46 percent of nineteen-year-old women had had sex; in the early 1970s, 53 percent; in the mid-1980s that number increased to 66 percent. Fewer than one in five nineteen-year-olds of either sex is a virgin today, and most young men and women have had sex for an average of eight years before they marry. Nearly three-fourths of the women who marry today have had more than one sexual partner, and 21 percent have had six or more.[1]

What do these statistics tell us? That in matters sexual, the "just say no" approach is not working. Part of the reason it is not working (if it is ever seriously suggested) is that there has been no strong positive offered as an alternative. The late Francis Schaeffer said that the two strongest drives in man are the sex drive and the desire to know God. Both are positive and both are powerful. But only one is able to fulfill our deepest longings. Sex is not the answer to the emptiness every man or woman feels at times in his or her heart. But a real and living relationship with our Creator through His Son, Jesus Christ, is.

LOOKING FOR LOVE

"SWM, good-looking, average H/W, mid-30s, seeks SWF, 25-30, never married, or divorced, no children, for fun, companionship, leading to serious relationship. I am kind, outgoing, dependable and honest—and I will treat you like a queen. No codependents or bitter victims, please. I am ready for love, and you should be too."

Do you read the personal ads? They provide a fascinating commentary on our times. But if I were seeking my true love, I would read them with a healthy skepticism. No matter what the writer of any personal ad may claim, he or she almost never gets down to the hard truth of the search. If they did, the personals would read more like this: "SWM seeks unconditional love. Desires wholeness, fulfillment, and complete acceptance from another person—preferably someone who is perfect but does not expect perfection from me.

Looking for that special someone to make me happy and satisfy all of my needs. Those with needs of their own need not reply."

Almost certainly the writer of the first ad is expecting the "SWF" he is seeking to fill his needs—and in all likelihood, that includes having sex with him. But a desire for sex is probably not the primary motive for placing his ad. More than anything, he wants to connect with someone. Many people who enter even the most casual sexual relationships are not promiscuous, but they are lonely. They want wholeness and acceptance and relationship, but they'll take sex instead—because it is pleasurable, and because they are not sure they'll ever *have* what they most desire, or even that there really *is* anything more.

G. K. Chesterton once argued that the man who knocks on the door of a brothel is knocking for God. In other words, within each of us there is a desire for the transcendent. We are more than bodies with physical hungers and responses. We are all looking for love…but love is not sex. Sex was designed as an expression of covenant love—the kind of love with which God loves us. Sexual intercourse in marriage is a microcosm of that covenant love. And that is the kind of connection we are hungry for.

Unfortunately, the transcendent is not easy to come by. In our culture of instant gratification, in our efficient-but-impersonal world, we are starving for the intimacy that comes from being deeply known, loved, and accepted. The renewed interest today in spirituality, particularly in new age religion (which is really age-old Eastern mysticism) reflects that hunger. We want something outside of ourselves, something bigger-than-life, something awe-inspiring to hold on to. But if we can't seem to find it, then sex is a likely substitute which will have to do.

Do you see what has happened? Sex—which was created to be a peak physical, emotional, and spiritual experience that reflects the transcendent relationship between God and man and is to be expressed in the most intimate of relationships between husband and wife—has become a kind of "existential pacifier" instead. It is *used* rather than *celebrated*. It actually prevents, in many cases, the development of the kind of intimacy it imitates. It is this kind of "bad sex" that ultimately drives out the good, as writer Tim Stafford notes: "When easy sex is available many do not wait and work for sex within a strong marriage. Commitments become a rarity, because people don't need them to gain sexual pleasure. By not depriving single people of bad sex, we end up depriving them of good sex."[2]

What is the bottom line? Just this: Sex outside of marriage is not the real thing. It is not pure sex, and no matter how physically gratifying it may seem, it is not great sex. It has more in common with a sneeze than a symphony. It bears less resemblance to the transcendent than does a Harlequin romance novel. Premarital sex is about as far from real intimacy as a flea circus is from a safari. So, instead of thinking of what you might be missing by saying no to premarital sex, think what you could be gaining by saying yes to a higher love, a higher freedom, and a higher call.

SAY YES TO A HIGHER LOVE

If you are among the majority of unmarried adults who is sexually active, let me encourage you to "just say yes" to building a solid foundation of relational intimacy and to make that intimacy—not physical lovemaking—the focus of your premarital relationships. Because without a foundation of real intimacy, any relationship you embark upon will be handicapped from the start and ultimately result in disappointment. Pure sex—total physical, emotional, and spiritual oneness—is simply too heavy to support with no foundation. It needs a solid relational base to bear its weight.

Let me illustrate. Have you ever seen Michelangelo's famous *David* (or a photograph of it)? The *David* stands in a modest-sized rotunda in a Florence, Italy, museum, beautifully elevated and bathed in natural light. It is impressive from any angle. The statue's lines are so fine that one almost expects to see a pulse quicken the smoothly chiseled veins in its neck and hands. Visitors to the Academe point to David's beautiful face, his fearless eyes, his powerful legs and shoulders. Almost no one comments on the tree stump that braces his right leg, but its presence is no mere ornamental afterthought—it is an essential part of the whole.

When the sculptor conceived his warrior-king, he knew the

powerful pose he desired to bring out of the quarried marble would not stand under its own weight. It needed something to brace it, to shore it up against itself. Without the half-hidden stump, Michelangelo's masterpiece would have toppled over centuries ago and been lost to future generations. But no one praises the artistry of the stump. No one thrills at its beauty. It is not the reason visitors stand in line for hours at this Florentine museum—but it is foundational to the *David*.

You see, Michelangelo knew his craft. He had not only the vision of an artistic genius, but the exacting patience and workmanship of a skilled laborer. In *David*, he created something that was not only breathtakingly beautiful, but a work that would stand the test of time. It would last. He knew the raw material—the marble—and what it could and could not do. He crafted the supporting stump with every bit as much passion and attention to detail as he did the lovely hand that sealed Goliath's fate.

Real, relational intimacy is the foundation for pure sex. It is a higher love than the physical intimacy people confuse for the real thing. Sex without relational intimacy is like a fragment of a masterpiece. Imagine viewing only the big toe of Michelangelo's famous sculpture in a sterile museum case. Separated from the whole its meaning would be lost, its majesty diminished. It needs to be viewed as a whole, and it needs a foundation to be fully expressed and enjoyed. How do you build relational intimacy? How do you construct a masterpiece of higher love? I believe there are four key components: time, talk, truth, and touch.

1. Time

Time is so important to the maturing of love. Too many couples rush into love without taking the time required to really know their partner. When bad-boy actor Charlie Sheen became engaged to *Elite* model Donna Peele, they had only just met. Sporting a huge diamond ring on her finger, Peele told the *New York Post,* "I know he has a bad reputation and I've only known him three and a half weeks, but I love him."[3]

They were married less than a year.

Real love takes time to grow. I dated Jo Beth for six years before we married. I can tell you that I loved her more on our wedding day than I did on our first date, and I love her more today, thirty-some-odd years later, than I did on our wedding day. Time is not the enemy of love. It is love's best friend.

On three separate occasions in the beautiful Song of Solomon, the king said of his bride-to-be: "I adjure you, O daughters of Jerusalem, by the gazelles or by the hinds of the field, that you will not arouse or awaken my love, until she pleases" (Song of Solomon 2:7; 3:5; 8:4). Solomon was completely enamored of this woman, yet he waited to fully express his love for her. He gave it time.

Are you willing to invest the time it takes to truly know and love another person? Until you are, you will never experience the kind of higher love that makes pure sex possible. "Time's not love's fool," wrote Shakespeare.[4] In every week, every month, every year that goes by, love deepens, trust grows, and understanding is nurtured. "Give it time" is some of the best advice I know for building relational intimacy.

2. Talk

Did you know that when couples see a therapist for sexual dysfunction or dissatisfaction, they are frequently told to stop having intercourse? That's right—they are told to postpone the physical expression of their love for a season and begin instead to really talk to one another, with touching allowed only in nonsexual ways. Those who communicate their love by sexual touch only are missing out on one of the most pleasurable, exciting expressions of intimacy available: talk.

Now, it is at this point that most men need to listen up and pay attention. You see, women are naturally talkative and conversational, whereas most men want to open up and share their hearts about as much as they want a root canal! However, talk is essential for a healthy, growing relationship. Furthermore, it must be intimate, heart-to-heart talk that expresses feelings and temperament as well as words.

Before the lovers in Song of Solomon touched one another, they wooed each other with passionate, loving words, and each listened intently to the other. The king said to his intended: "To me, my darling, you are like my mare among the chariots of Pharaoh. Your cheeks are lovely with ornaments, your neck with strings of beads" (Song of Solomon 1:9–10). Today, that might sound something like this: "Darling, there is nothing in the world as fine and precious to me as you are. You are so beautiful, and I love to look at you and know that you are mine."

And then, "How beautiful you are, my darling, how beautiful you are!... You have made my heart beat faster, my sister, my bride.... You are a garden spring, a well of fresh water, and streams flowing from Lebanon" (Song of Solomon 4:1, 9, 15). Or, as a modern lover might say: "Honey, just seeing you makes my heart race. There is no other woman in the world who is more beautiful to me. Being with you is always fresh and exciting. And when you're next to me, I feel like a king."

Likewise, the Shulammite woman said to her king: "Like an apple tree among the trees of the forest, so is my beloved among the young men.... He has brought me to his banquet hall, and his banner over me is love" (Song of Solomon 2:3–4). Or, "Honey, you are one of a kind—and there is no other man who even comes close to you in my eyes! With you in my life I am rich beyond compare...and your love is my favorite thing to wear!"

Then later, "His mouth is full of sweetness. And he is wholly desirable. This is my beloved and this is my friend" (Song of Solomon 5:16). In other words: "Your kisses are so incredible! I love to get close to you and I want you so much. But you're not just my lover—you're my best friend in the whole world."

"I could never say anything like that," some might protest. "How embarrassing." But then, we can undress one another and have intercourse as if it were nothing at all. Talk is intimate, too, and the fact that many find it easier to have sex than to initiate a deep conversation speaks volumes about their relationships. Why would you believe that you could have an intimate relationship with someone to whom you have nothing to say? A higher love is built on talk—and lots of it.

What should you talk about? Talk about your past—about what brought you to the place where you are today. Talk about your family and friends and about other relationships that are important to you. Talk about your beliefs and about what matters most to you in life. Talk about God and what His love means to you. Talk about your dreams and goals for the future. Talk about what makes you happy or sad. And share how you feel about each other.

In fact, a good rule of thumb for the physical expression of intimacy in a relationship is that you should never say with your body anything you have not said, or cannot say, verbally. The problem with sex outside of marriage is not that we get naked—it's that we don't get naked *enough*. Real intimacy involves your heart, your soul, your flesh, your psyche, your self-worth, your mind, your spirit. Talking about all of this keeps us honest and lays another choice stone in the foundation of a higher love.

3. Truth

Genuine relational intimacy is impossible apart from the truth. Nothing lasting can be built upon a foundation of dishonesty. Are you a truth teller? Do you say what you mean and mean what you say? Are you trustworthy? Can others count on your word? Real love is truthful, and it "speaks the truth in love" (Ephesians 4:15). I am amazed today by the proliferation of private investigators whose practice consists of checking up on men whose wives or girlfriends do not trust them. For a fee, they track down and stake out the suspect partner and report on his actions. For the record, I am not being sexist. Nine times out of ten, it is women who feel the need to test the integrity of the men in their lives, and not the reverse. Where trust is absent, truth usually has been compromised.

It takes the first two elements of relational intimacy—time and talk—to build up the third element of truth. Where truth is present, you can be sure that love is genuine. Truth is a hallmark of the real thing. "Little children," the apostle John wrote, "let us not love with word or with tongue, but in deed and truth" (1 John 3:18). Once the truth has been compromised, it is difficult to regain the trust that is so critical to a growing, healthy relationship.

4. Touch

The final element of relational intimacy is meaningful touch. Time, talk, and truth establish a safe atmosphere where touch that means something can be enjoyed. Casual sex destroys the pleasure of meaningful touch the way too many sweets spoil the pleasure of a good meal. It is hard to appreciate the delights of the five food groups when you're on a sugar high!

One author has rightly stated that we are a culture that has gone from the innocence of "I wanna hold your hand" to the crudeness of "I want your sex." We've lost the joy and innocence of touching the one we love in a way that communicates not a selfish desire for gratification, but appreciation and wonder. There is a kind of hierarchy of touch that is often observed by couples in love. It begins with hand to hand touching, then moves from hand to shoulder, then hand to waist. Each step conveys increasing levels of intimacy. From hand to waist touching, couples move to kissing—first in a casual, affectionate way, and later in a deeper, more passionate way. Hand to breast touching frequently follows deep kissing, then hand to genital touching, and finally, genital to genital touching that culminates in sexual intercourse. Within each of these stages, there are countless varieties and subtleties of expression available.

Unfortunately, we've become so jaded by the media, early sexual experiences, and exposure to all kinds of sexual images, that we're hardly able to appreciate the thrill of brushing a hand across a loved one's cheek, or feeling fingers intertwined. These simple pleasures of touch need to be reclaimed and our taste for them renewed, if we are to know true relational intimacy. A tender kiss on the movie screen used to be incredibly stirring, but today a screen kiss is likely to be lost in a blur of nudity and explicit sexual activity. The kind of higher love we need to say yes to includes tender touch that conveys deep meaning.

Time, talk, truth, and touch are all aspects of this higher love. While the Bible doesn't define love very simply, it does illustrate it beautifully: "Love is patient, love is kind, and is not jealous; love does not brag and is not arrogant, does not act unbecomingly; it does not seek its own, is not provoked, does not take into account a wrong suffered, does not rejoice in unrighteousness, but rejoices with the truth; bears all things, believes all things, hopes all things, endures all things" (1 Corinthians 13:4–7; also see chapter 5). Real love is self-giving. It is sacrificial. It is volitional. It involves a choice, an act of the will. It is not quick, cheap, or easy. But it is a work of art as sure as Michelangelo's famous sculpture—and its foundation is what makes its lasting loveliness possible.

SAY YES TO A HIGHER FREEDOM

All three of my sons played basketball. When they were growing up, they frequently wanted me to drive them to various recreational parks around our city where they knew some tough pick-up games were played. Naturally, they didn't want to be seen with Dad, so I'd drive them a little way from the court, let them out of the car, and then come around on my own a few minutes later to watch.

One evening I took one of the boys to a lighted court a few minutes from our house. I let him out, then went and watched two half-court games nearby. The two games could not have been more different from one another. On one end of the court it was a free-for-all. I mean, it must have been basketball they were playing because the familiar round ball was there—but that's where the resemblance to the game I know ended. It looked more like a combination of football, rugby, and wrestling. I am sure the original object was to get the ball through the hoop, but that quickly became secondary to winning the shoving, cussing, and trash-talking matches that were going on. No rules. No regulations. No whistles. No fouls.

And no fun.

At the other end of the same court, a smooth, sharp game was in progress. These guys were players. They handled the ball like you would not believe. They knew what a foul was and even called a few on themselves! They understood hand-checking and blocking out. They were doing some simply amazing passing and rebounding. This was a skilled game, no doubt about it. With the talent they exhibited, these guys were going somewhere, and their high-flying, above-the-rim kind of basketball was a thrill to behold.

Now, let me ask you something: If you were a real player, which game would you want to be in? The one with no rules and little skill? I don't think so. If you had any talent at all, that game would do nothing but frustrate you, and your chances of being seriously injured would be high. But down at the other end of the court, you could shine. The disciplined game would give you the chance to make some precise passes, sharpen your ball handling, and learn how to execute the perfect pick and roll. If you were a real player, that's where you would want to be. The game with no rules would inhibit your freedom to excel, but the disciplined game would give you all the freedom you need to play well.

In just the same way, you can have a higher freedom sexually when you choose to honor the rules of the game. I can guarantee you the person who decides to live inside some very simple, plain, and clear guidelines drawn by God for his or her sexuality will know more freedom than the one who ignores them. "The experience of freedom has to do with being loved and loving," writes psychiatrist John White. "God designed you because He loved you. His purposes for you are an expression of His love to you. As you respond in love to His commands (about sex or anything else), you are set free—free to be and do what both you and God want. The more completely you are enslaved in love to His blessed will, the freer you will discover yourself to be."[5]

The truth is, what most think will satisfy—that is, pleasure seeking with no boundaries—will not. What the freedom lover discovers instead is that "living for pleasure is the least pleasurable thing a man can do. If his neighbors don't kill him in disgust, he will die slowly of boredom and powerlessness."[6] It is what we are afraid will limit us that will truly set us free. The truest freedom you or I could experience is the freedom that most closely conforms with our true nature—and our true nature is God-breathed and God-designed. He knows best how we are to function in the universe He made and set into motion. Say yes to a higher freedom by living inside the parameters established by God for your sexuality.

SAY YES TO A HIGHER CALL

True relational intimacy is achieved by saying yes to a higher call. What is that call? To glorify God rather than to satisfy self. The apostle Paul wrote to Timothy, his younger brother in the faith: "Now flee from youthful lusts, and pursue righteousness, faith, love and peace, with those who call on the Lord from a pure heart" (2 Timothy 2:22). Paul's advice was not just that Timothy run *from* immorality, but that he run *to* something better. What did he recommend that Timothy pursue? Righteousness, or rightness in God's eyes. Faith. Real love. Peace. He also advised him to pursue those things in the company of others who loved and depended on God as he did.

If you make it your aim to pursue righteousness, love, and peace in this life, and if you surround yourself with others who are pursuing those same things out of a genuine love for God, I can promise that you will have fewer struggles with sexual temptation than those who live to please themselves.

If you are a Christian, you know that your body is the very temple in which God's Holy Spirit dwells. Your call, then, is to surrender it, along with your will, to the lordship of Jesus Christ. "Or do you not know that your body is a temple of the Holy Spirit who is in you, whom you have from God, and that you are not your own? For you have been bought with a price: therefore glorify God in your body" (1 Corinthians 6:19–20).

You cannot glorify God in your body by participating in sexual intercourse outside of marriage. If you are unmarried, you glorify God in your body by remaining celibate. If you are married, you glorify God in your body by sexual fidelity to your mate. Either celibacy or fidelity. It's that simple.

Say yes to a higher call. Determine that you belong to God—you are His possession—and that you will not unite your body with anyone but your marriage partner. Instead of seeking to satisfy your sexual desires, decide to pursue instead the characteristics of righteousness, love, and peace. When you do this, you are embarking on the best possible preparation for achieving relational intimacy. And you will be learning from the very Master of intimacy Himself.

WHAT IF I'VE REALLY BLOWN IT?

If you have been sexually involved outside of marriage, once or many times, or if you are having sex now as a single person, I have a few words especially for you. First, you have a choice. What you do with your sexuality from this point forward is up to you. It is never too late to begin doing the right thing. You can decide today to honor your own nature, your future mate if you marry, and God, by abstaining from sexual intercourse, starting now. As impossible as that may seem, Jesus Christ can give you the power to do it. Not for the sake of denial, but for the sake of something better. I know many, many people who, by the grace of God, waited for marriage to experience sex with their mate, and not a single one of them has ever expressed regret about that fact.

If you are carrying around a great deal of guilt about your sexual past, you have a choice there too. You can try to cover it up or deny it, or you can confess it to God and receive His forgiveness. You can start over! The Bible says "If we confess our sins, He is faithful and righteous to forgive us our sins and to cleanse us from all unrighteousness" (1 John 1:9). And when God forgives sin, He does not just agree to overlook it, He remembers it no more! He forgives ...and forgets.

Finally, you have a choice about how you will seek to fill your deepest longings for love and intimacy. Let me share with you a story that I believe contains the answer. It's about a woman with a past and a man with an offer that sounded too good to be true. Her name is not recorded. In fact, all we know about her at the beginning of the story is that she was a Samaritan, a race especially hated by Jews. But on this particular afternoon, by a small well in a town called Sychar, she met a young Jewish teacher who asked her for water. "Give me a drink," He said.

When the shock of His addressing her wore off, she said to Him, "How is it that You, being a Jew, ask me for a drink since I am a Samaritan woman?"

His reply carried deeper meaning than she could possibly know, because He was not just any teacher, but Jesus the Messiah, the very

Son of God Himself. "If you knew the gift of God," He said, "and who it is who says to you, 'Give Me a drink,' you would have asked Him, and He would have given you living water."

He was speaking in figurative language of spiritual things, but she was earthly minded. "Sir," she reasoned. "You have nothing to draw with and the well is deep; where then do You get that living water?"

He recognized her confusion but held firm to His original offer: "Everyone who drinks of this water shall thirst again; but whoever drinks of the water that I shall give him shall never thirst; but the water that I shall give him shall become in him a well of water springing up to eternal life."

"Sir," she replied, "give me this water, so I will not be thirsty, nor come all the way here to draw."

At that, He stunned her with a bolt out of the blue: "Go, call your husband, and come here." She had no husband—but she had previously had several and did have a current lover.

"I have no husband," she answered, probably thinking that it was wise to end the conversation here.

But He already knew the shambles she had made of her love life, and it did not cause Him to recoil from her or to withdraw His generous (if mysterious) offer. It stood. When she decided to broach a safer topic with Him (like religion!) and began to speculate about the Messiah, He stunned her yet again by saying, "I am He."

Five husbands and a lover had not satisfied her thirst for love and intimacy, but Jesus offered something that would: living water. A spring that would flow inside her very soul and bring with it the promise of eternal life. A source of love that was constant and clean and not dependent on any man or human relationship.

Did she accept the offer? I believe that she did. The Bible tells us that she was so overwhelmed with the amazing promise of living water that she left the pot she came to fill and went into the city telling everyone she met, "Come, see a man who told me all the things that I have done; this is not the Christ, is it?" It was indeed.

Do you need a place to take your sexual past? Take it to Him. Do you need unconditional love and acceptance and real relational intimacy? Receive them from Him. Have you looked everywhere for an answer to the emptiness in your soul, only to find it growing deeper still? Come and see a man who knows everything you've ever done and yet loves you with a love so perfect it can quench every thirst and cover every sin. Just say yes to the greatest lover the world has ever known. His name is Jesus. He alone is the One who fills the emptiness of our lives, ends the sadness of our searching, and gives us the kind of pure love that will make our relationships truly satisfying.

CHAPTER NINE

Gay Sex

So What's the Problem?

King Solomon wrote in the Book of Ecclesiastes that "there is nothing new under the sun," and that is true sexually as well as philosophically. Homosexual behavior is not new. But in late twentieth-century America, it has attained a level of cultural acceptance never before enjoyed in this country. What was once regarded as aberrant sexual behavior is now supported as a viable lifestyle. Men and women who desire sexual relations only with those of their own gender are termed "homosexual" or "gay" persons, and they claim that heterosexual relations are outside their natural "orientation."

But who defines what is "natural"? Our relativistic culture, or something more solid than the shifting sands of social mores? When the apostle Paul condemns the practice of homosexual acts, his assumptions of what is normal or natural are based on God's revelation—especially in His creation of men and women and of their sexual union as recorded in Genesis. "This can be juxtaposed to and compared with our contemporary ideas about what is natural," writes Tim Stafford, "but neither source of revelation is able to contradict the other, because they spring from utterly different premises.

In the end, one must choose which source—Scripture or contemporary experience—to trust."[1]

The Bible states clearly that the practice of homosexual behavior is a sexual perversion. It is forbidden specifically in both the Old and New Testaments (Genesis 19:1–20; Leviticus 18:22; 20:13; Judges 19:1–25; Romans 1:24–27; 1 Corinthians 6:9–11; and 1 Timothy 1:9–11). The Bible does not call homosexuality an alternative lifestyle; it calls it an abomination. A sin.

Homosexuality is not a special case nor the worst of all compulsions, but it may be the most misunderstood and insidious of all the sexually addictive behaviors. I address it here because so many in our culture are caught in its trap and because the church has been polarized in its response to the problem, tending either to ignore it altogether or to compromise scriptural standards to accommodate its practice.

I understand that the Bible's view (and therefore my own) of homosexual behavior is not popular or politically correct. I know that everyone from Dear Abby to Dennis Rodman disagrees with my position. Today's modern, individualistic morality argues that nothing is sinful so long as it does not immediately harm another—but that is simply not true. Homosexuality is a form of idolatry, as is every sin, and that alone qualifies it as wrong. "You shall have no other gods before Me," God commanded His people (Exodus 20:3). But modern man does not want God telling him what to do—especially with his genitals. Instead, "we will suffer almost anything, even death it seems, to avoid accepting the yoke of heaven."[2]

There is a strong, vocal, and thus far relatively successful movement afoot to "normalize" homosexuality. But homosexuality is not normal, and the lifestyle surrounding it is far from gay. The reality of the practicing homosexual is light years removed from the sanitized version depicted by mainstream media and gay rights proponents. Consider the following risks associated with homosexual behavior:

- a significantly decreased likelihood of establishing or preserving a successful marriage

- a twenty-five- to thirty-year decrease in life expectancy

- chronic, potentially fatal liver disease (infectious hepatitis) which increases the risk of liver cancer

- inevitably fatal immune disease, including associated cancers

- a high frequency of fatal rectal cancer

- multiple bowel and other infectious diseases

- a much higher than average incidence of suicide[3]

Does this sound happy? I can assure you that the vast majority of those who are practicing homosexuality are far from gay. I also believe many homosexuals long to be free of their behavior and even of their same-sex desires. But because the reality of this so-called lifestyle is obscured by a number of myths that have come to be accepted by many as fact, homosexuals desiring to change are frequently discouraged from attempting to do so.

SIX MYTHS ABOUT HOMOSEXUALITY

First, as the statistics above dispute, there is the myth that *homosexuality is a very normal, comfortable, healthy (and even desirable) lifestyle.* In truth, less than 2 percent of homosexuals live to be sixty-five years of age, although normal life expectancy in this country is well into the seventies for both men and women. In fact, the median age of death for the homosexual male is thirty-eight, and for lesbians it is forty-five. One rigorous study of nearly five thousand homosexual men reported that 69 to 83 percent had had more than fifty lifetime sexual partners, and over 80 percent had engaged in receptive anal intercourse with at least some of their partners in the previous two years.[4]

Another study revealed that only 2 percent of homosexuals were monogamous or semimonogamous—generously defined as having ten or fewer lifetime partners. And a 1978 study found that 43 percent of male homosexuals estimated having sex with five hundred or more different partners, and 28 percent with a thousand or more.[5]

Another myth about homosexuality revolves around the numbers game, and the frequently quoted statistic *that 10 percent of the male population in America is homosexual.* That statistic dates back to the Kinsey Report and is questionable, at best. The recent University of Chicago study found a nationwide incidence of male homosexuality of only 2.8 percent, and of female homosexuality only 1.4 percent, and although the sample size was small, this is a significant discrepancy from the oft-quoted "one out of ten."

The third widely propagated myth about homosexuality is that *opposition to the practice of homosexuality is always the result of homophobia or hatred.* All who oppose the practice of homosexuality are not categorically driven by ignorance, small mindedness, fear, or hatred. Homosexuality is not a political issue, or a civil rights issue, or even a tolerance issue at heart, although gay rights activists have certainly sought to make it so. It is a moral issue. And to oppose homosexual practice on moral grounds is a thoroughly defensible position.

Homosexuality is often the last outpost of sexual perversion to be sanctioned in a society that has set aside all other sexual constraints, and when those constraints are lost, history has proven that civilization suffers. Opposing homosexuality does not automatically make one a hater of people who practice it, a narrow-minded bigot, or a mean-spirited zealot. It is possible—in fact it is absolutely necessary—to love the practicing homosexual but hate his or her acts. The distinction is critical. "We must decide how to best counter the tactics of intimidation and refute the false claims of a group that operates in the hostile mode of raw, power politics," writes Dr. Jeffrey Satinover, while at the same time, "retain the profound compassion and fellow-feeling toward individual homosexuals that we ourselves need and yearn for from others."[6] It is the responsibility of every Christian to love those who are struggling, no matter what their struggle involves. The fact that our neighbor calls himself a homosexual does not represent a "holy loophole" in Christ's command that we love one another.

Probably the most hotly debated myth regarding homosexuality at present is the myth that *homosexuality is inherited,* or that there is a "gay gene" that causes homosexual orientation. When a 1993 study in *Science* suggested the link between genetics and homosexuality, the media readily seized on the story with enthusiasm. The *Wall Street Journal* trumpeted that "Research Points toward a Gay Gene."[7] Easily ignored amid the hype was a brief quote from a noted geneticist who expressed reservations, saying the incidence of the Xq28 gene among homosexual men might well be associational, not causal. National Public Radio "scooped" the story the day before its publication with the celebratory announcement that scientists had discovered the gene that causes homosexuality, and the *New York Times* headline read "Report Suggests Homosexuality Is Linked to Genes," while the text of the very same article warned against "over-interpretation" of the data.

Since 1993, the consensus of the scientific community is that the gay gene research done by Dean Hamer and his colleagues is inconclusive with regard to cause. Some go further, suggesting that the idea that a gay gene even *influences* male homosexual behavior is something of a stretch. Four months after the original study appeared in its own pages, *Science* ran another article critical of the assumptions on which it was based and on its questionable interpretation of statistics. Sadly (but not surprisingly), that second article received little or no media fanfare.

If homosexuality is not inherited, then what *does* cause it? The answer, which few of us are willing to admit, is this: *No one really knows.* There do seem to be, however, certain circumstances and pressures that can cause a man or woman to conclude "I am gay." What I have found to be true of nearly every homosexual person I have known is that homosexual orientation is not something people *seek.* In fact, most would willingly choose to deal with any other problem, addiction, or compulsion than homosexuality.

What are some of the common factors in the background of those struggling with homosexuality? First, a disruption in their relationship with the parent of the same sex, either by absence, rejection, or emotional distancing. (I have yet to meet a homosexual man who claimed a solid, loving relationship with his father.) Second, many who call themselves homosexual possess a sensitive disposition, a strong, creative bent, and a keen aesthetic sense.

Perhaps as a result of the difficulties of the same-sex parent relationship, many homosexuals report a deep longing for father or mother nurturing that is later transferred to peers or older members of their sex. When puberty arrives, it is nearly inevitable that these desires will become confused and intermingled with the natural emerging sexual desires of the individual. Many homosexuals also report high incidences of childhood molestation or incest or of having been exposed to homoerotic influences early in life.

At some point, the young person gives in to his or her longings (which are not necessarily sexual) and begins to have voluntary homosexual experiences. What he finds is that sex—any kind of sex—can be a powerful drug to a person in pain. The high of orgasm and sexual release temporarily relieve distresses of all sorts, and a cycle begins that eventually makes homosexual behavior the central "organizing" factor in life.

Related to the genetic myth is the myth that *homosexual desire necessitates homosexual behavior.* Both of these arguments are veiled attempts to deny the individual's personal responsibility for his or her chosen lifestyle. The argument that homosexuality cannot be immoral because it is genetic (although unproven) is the ultimate cop-out and is usually followed by the insistence that an individual must practice the orientation that he or she has been dealt by nature. (It is ironic that feminists—the frequent political allies of homosexuals and their causes—argue vehemently against the idea that their physiology in any way dictates or limits their behavior, and yet this is the very theory that proponents of homosexuality rush to embrace!)

The problem with this myth is that man is born with a free will and the latitude to exercise it. A man or woman with homosexual desires does not have to practice homosexual behavior any more than someone with a bent toward alcoholism has to drink, or that someone with heterosexual desires has to be sexually active! It is not inevitable. In most areas of life, people fight passionately for personal freedom and choice, but many gay activists seem to want personal freedom only if it's freedom to sin. They are fiercely determined to prove there is no way out of their compulsive sexual practices.

Finally, it is a myth that *homosexuality is immutable,* that a homosexual cannot alter his desires or behavior. That is more than a myth. It is a lie. I know many former homosexuals who, through their own desire and commitment, the power of the indwelling Christ, and the help of family, friends, and counselors, have abandoned the homosexual life. Some are married. Many are not. But all would tell you that change—healing—is possible. That there is hope. As with any addiction, sexual or otherwise, homosexuality will not just go away because the homosexual wants it to disappear. It requires confession, repentance, healing, and accountability.

The way out is not easy. If it were, more would have chosen it. Not only does it demand great determination and spiritual discipline, it often means the loss of many of the former homosexual's closest relationships and his or her only known support system. But it can be done. Despite the unpopularity of the notion in the militantly gay community, many groups and individuals do "treat" those desiring to be free of homosexuality with remarkable success. Sex researchers Masters and Johnson reported in their book *Homosexuality in Perspective* that in a study of eighty-one gays desiring "reorientation," 71.6 percent had been successful after six years.[8] Another nine-year study of male homosexuality concluded that "the therapeutic results of our study provide reason for an optimistic outlook. Many homosexuals become exclusively heterosexual in psychoanalytic treatment. In our judgment, a heterosexual shift is a possibility for all homosexuals who are strongly motivated to change."[9]

The way out is a process and it is long, but the rewards are tremendous. Groups under the Exodus International umbrella— including Homosexuals Anonymous, Desert Stream, Redeemed Life, and Pastoral Care Ministries—offer help from a Christian perspective but emphasize the need for the homosexual to truly desire healing and change.

If you or someone you know is struggling with homosexuality, take heart. Healing is possible. Even though "the course to full restoration of heterosexuality typically lasts longer than the average American marriage,"[10] the road to wholeness itself can prove extraordinarily fulfilling. Understand that there is no shame in struggle. And there is no shame in being broken on God's anvil. Ask Jacob—whose late night wrestling match with God's angel left him limping for life, but a better man. Or quiz David—whose sexual sins scarred generations of his family but whose passion for God became the hallmark of his life. We struggle because, while we are end-result people, our God is a process God. We want the gold star that says we've arrived once and for all, but He delights in every tiny step of obedience we take along the way. "The battle for obedience," writes John Piper, "is the fight of faith. That's why the only fight we fight is the fight of faith. We fight to be so satisfied with all that God is for us in Jesus that temptation to sin loses its power over us."[11]

Ancient Greek poetry records the story of Odysseus and of the sirens—mythical, evil creatures, half-bird and half-woman. The sirens lived on an island surrounded by submerged, jagged rocks, and as ships approached, they would sing beautiful, seductive songs to lure the sailors to their death upon the rocks. When the ship of Odysseus approached, he reckoned on the strong pull of the sirens' music and ordered his crew to fill their ears with wax to mute the songs. This done, he commanded them to bind him to the mast as they passed the island, so that he himself would not be tempted to reverse his life-saving orders.

In a different myth, another traveler named Orpheus sang a song of his own that was so beautiful and divine his sailors did not even want to hear the sirens' music!

Sexual temptation is as alluring as the sirens' song—and certainly as persistent and dangerous. To escape it, we must not only fight against its compelling draw, but put in its place a stronger desire. We must learn to love a better song—a more beautiful melody than the one that would dash our lives on the rocks of sin.

No matter how difficult the task or how determined the opposition, the struggle itself can be glorious and joyful. Even when we feel that God is standing still, He is always moving toward us and intervening to restore us to full fellowship with Him. That is His nature—and the nature of His pure love. We must choose to tune our hearts to His song—to His voice—and to believe in the power and beauty of His truth. His question to the homosexual is no different from the one He would ask you or me: "Who do you believe? Who do you trust?" Trust Him. His way works.

CHAPTER TEN

Sexual Chaos

Dealing with Sexual Addiction

P olice in Harlingen, Texas, arrested nine teenage gang members in 1994 who took part in a brutal, two-hour sexual assault on a young woman they abducted at gunpoint. She knew none of the attackers, who raped and sodomized her more than half a dozen times. They ranged in age from fourteen to sixteen.

Nearly 140,000 children under the age of eighteen are sexually abused by their parents or caretakers each year in the United States.[1]

AIDS is now the leading cause of death among Americans age twenty-five to forty-four, according to the Federal Centers for Disease Control and Prevention in Atlanta, Georgia.[2]

The pornography industry in this country is estimated to be worth $4 to $5 billion, making it larger than the commercial movie and recording industries combined.[3]

Computer technology has ushered in "user-friendly" cybersex. In an eighteen-month study, researchers at Carnegie Mellon University found 917,410 sexually explicit pictures, short stories, and film clips on-line.[4]

Soft porn has invaded mainstream publishing, as demonstrated by two recent books offered by Random House. The first consisted of a "long transcription of an entirely satisfying anonymous phone sex relationship"; the second was the story of a man who discovers he can freeze time by snapping his fingers. When time is frozen, he takes the clothes off of unresisting women and masturbates. Available for a suggested retail price of $21, without a brown paper wrapper, at your local (nonadult) bookstore.[5]

Researchers now conclude that one in four Americans grapple with some form of sexual addiction—and that one out of every ten *Christians* is involved in sexual addiction.[6] Clearly, something has gone wrong with our sexual appetites.

The terrifying thing, the truly horrifying thing, is not simply that these perversions are taking place, but that they are by and large considered normal. They are routinely accepted (or at least tolerated) by our politically correct, morally numb culture. Half a century ago, C. S. Lewis noted that "public opinion is less hostile to illicit unions and even to perversion than it has been since Pagan times."[7] That was in 1943. Lewis never witnessed the end of the twentieth century.

SEXUAL CHAOS

Welcome to the age of incest, voyeurism, prostitution, pornography, cybersex, phone sex, pedophilia, and other paraphilias. Welcome to the age of indulgence and obsession where any sexual act, no matter how wicked, is deemed no reason for shame. Or is it?

If sex is good and God-created, when *should* we be ashamed of our runaway sexual appetites? Is there a point where a good thing becomes bad? Psychiatrist and author John White says that "legitimate, God-given desire becomes lust the moment we make a god of it. To worship food is lust. To be neurotic about getting our full quota of sleep becomes sleep lust. To be enslaved to erotic sensations represents sexual lust."[8]

Lust is placing primary importance on a secondary thing. It is like a thirsty man's taste for salt: The more he feeds it, the thirstier he becomes, because the dirty secret of lust is that it never satisfies. C. S. Lewis illustrated this beautifully in his *Chronicles of Narnia*. When Edmund, one of the four Pevensie children who discover the land of Narnia through an old wardrobe, meets the evil White Witch, she tempts him with a treat called "Turkish Delight." The taste of it is so wonderful it brings him completely under her spell. But Edmund eventually learns that while Turkish Delight is momentarily delicious, it cannot ever satisfy. In fact, "anyone who had once tasted it would want more and more of it, and would even, if they were allowed, go on eating it till they killed themselves."[9]

When sexual desire becomes isolated from the rest of life and the drive for its satisfaction becomes a "primary thing," it is as wickedly irresistible and unsatisfying as Edmund's Turkish Delight. And worst of all, it ruins our taste for *true* delight. "He [Edmund] had eaten his share of the dinner but hadn't really enjoyed it because he was thinking all the time about Turkish Delight—and there's nothing that spoils the taste of good ordinary food half so much as the memory of bad magic food."[10]

There's something enticing about forbidden fruit, isn't there? There is an inexplicable lure toward what is prohibited. Adam and Eve had all that paradise could offer and certainly more fruit than they could sample in a lifetime. But they were drawn like iron shavings to a magnet to the one piece of fruit that God said they should not taste. We are no different. It begins when we are children and a parent says, "No candy before dinner." Why is candy eaten before dinner so delicious? Why is it suddenly more desirable than candy eaten at any other time?

Unfortunately, we don't outgrow our passion for the forbidden. What does the typical adult with a high cholesterol count crave? Ice cream. French fries. And the corner fast food restaurant seems so much more appealing than the produce section of the grocery store. Soon "just a taste" or "just this once" becomes "oh, why not?" then "make mine supersized." We don't see the harm until we're in over our heads.

THE CYCLE OF ADDICTION

Addictions, even sexual addictions, are nothing new. In fact, the Bible tells us there is "nothing new under the sun" (Ecclesiastes 1:9). One of the most renowned judges in all of ancient Israel was very likely a sexual addict. His name was Samson. One historical writer said of him, "Samson…strangled a lion, but he could not strangle his own love. He burst the fetters of his foes; but not the cords of his own lusts."[11] Mighty Samson had a weakness, an Achilles heel. He lusted after nearly every attractive woman he saw. First he took for himself a Philistine woman from Timnah, then a prostitute from Gaza, and finally Delilah, who was his ultimate downfall. His story illustrates the typical cycle of addiction that applies to many areas, although Samson's addiction was sexual in nature.

1. Fantasy

Samson saw the Philistine woman and asked his Israelite parents to get her for him as a wife. He made this request in spite of the fact that God had forbidden intermarriage between Israel and her neighbors. His rationale? She looked good to him. He saw her…and he kept seeing her in his mind, replaying her image over and over again, and wanting her more with each "rerun." Fantasy is an escape. Many addicts fantasize to alleviate stress or to substitute for meeting legitimate needs. Fantasy promises everything to a man and asks nothing of him. "There's nothing wrong with imagining," some might argue, but fantasizing on the object of our lust only leads further and further downward into the spiral of addiction.

2. Ritualization

Most addicts have a ritual they perform before they actually give in to their particular addiction. Samson apparently "cruised" strange places looking at foreign or forbidden women. Although he was just looking, this was the first step in his ritual whose eventual end was sex. Gary Inrig writes, "We do not fall off a cliff morally, we go down a toboggan slope, until finally we are going so fast that we cannot stop. In many ways the critical issue is not what happens at the bottom of the toboggan run, or even halfway down. Once we start down, we can only bail out by drastic action. It is the first steps that are determinative. That is why personal purity is such a critical issue…. To compromise, even in our thought lives, makes us very vulnerable."[12]

3. Realization

In this stage the addiction is "realized" or acted out. When people act out their addiction, they are essentially saying to God, "You cannot or will not meet my deepest longings, so I'll do it on my own." Sooner or later, all continuing fantasy or ritual is acted upon. That is why this is not the stage to attempt to overcome addiction, although acting out one's fantasies needs to cease. The cycle of addiction must be arrested when one begins to feed the fantasy. The fantasy must be starved and ritualization replaced with new, healthy behaviors. "Abstinence is not the cure," one expert argues, "but merely its precondition. So long as people allow themselves the habitual, compulsive, self-soothing behavior for which they seek treatment, they will have an escape from the underlying emotional distress that prompts the repeated acting out during the first place."[13]

Perhaps Samson told himself he had business to conduct in Gaza. Then once he was there, he may have strolled down the streets where the temple prostitutes lingered. The first time he may only have looked. Then perhaps he spoke to one or two of these women. On his next business trip, he began to realize his addiction; he slept with one of the prostitutes. Oh, he probably swore he'd never do it again—called it a one-night stand, and put it behind him...until next time.

4. Paralysis

Repeated instances of realization or acting out lead to a stage of seeming paralysis. The addictive behavior becomes so deeply entrenched that the addict feels he no longer has a choice about his actions. By the time he began his disastrous liaison with Delilah, Samson had probably ceased to struggle against all sexual entanglements. As strong as he was, he seemed convinced that the lure of strange women was beyond his ability to withstand.

The first few acts may not produce paralysis, but after several more times the behavior becomes so deeply etched in the addict's mind that he feels he has no power to choose. Samson went through the ritual of returning to Gaza, then repeatedly realized his fantasy and was paralyzed.

5. Desensitization

Eventually, the addict becomes desensitized to the effects of sin. At this point, most addicts are more willing to change or adapt their career, their relationships, their commitments, and their beliefs to their addictions, than vice versa. Samson exemplified this. He felt bulletproof, even though he was not. By the time he received his famous haircut in the lap of Delilah, he was powerless—but completely unaware that the Spirit of God had left him. His conscience was seared.

The apostle Paul describes this very result in his letter to the Christians of ancient Rome: "Therefore God gave them over in the lusts of their hearts to impurity, that their bodies might be dishonored among them. For they exchanged the truth of God for a lie, and worshiped and served the creature rather than the Creator, who is blessed forever. Amen. For this reason God gave them over to degrading passions; for their women exchanged the natural function for that which is unnatural, and in the same way also the men abandoned the natural function of the woman and burned in their desire toward one another, men with men committing indecent acts and receiving in their own persons the due penalty of their error. And just as they did not see fit to acknowledge God any longer, God gave them over to a depraved mind, to do those things which are not proper" (Romans 1:24–28). God finally allowed them to suffer the inevitable consequences of what they continually chose. He does the same with us.

Although there are many sexual addictions, three in particular seem to plague our contemporary culture. They are pornography, sexual abuse, and homosexuality. We will look briefly here at pornography and sexual abuse (since homosexuality was addressed in the previous chapter), then consider how these and other addictions can be overcome.

THE ADDICTION OF PORNOGRAPHY

Pornography is difficult to define these days, but most of its proponents and opponents would probably agree that pornography is the display or description of sexual activity or nudity, meant to excite sexual feelings in viewers or readers. Obviously, all nudity is not pornography. Many museums around the world display great works of art depicting nudity, and they would not be considered pornographic. But certain magazines, movies, television shows, and books display sexuality in unhealthy and immoral ways and are *designed* to elicit sexual response.

Pornography, along with fantasy and masturbation, is considered one of the three "building blocks" of sexual addiction. These activities work together to form a cycle that is difficult to break. "Fantasy is created by a need to satisfy deep longings. Pornography displays images of how to do that. Masturbation is the physical expression.... Pornography stimulates fantasy. Fantasy needs to be expressed. Masturbation allows a release of that need."[14] While this cycle may temporarily satisfy a physical need for sexual release, it never satisfies the emotional and spiritual hunger of the sexual addict's soul.

Pornography, too, provides an escape from real life. Many argue that it is harmless and hurts no one else. This is a lie. Porn addicts never learn to satisfy their sexual hunger in a healthy way. The cycle becomes degenerative. It gets worse and worse. Their relationships suffer, and they become increasingly isolated. And the insidious messages of pornography subtly teach a devalued view of women (or men) and an unrealistic view of relationships, romance, intimacy, and sexuality.

Unfortunately, pornography is becoming more and more accessible. Mass-market cable companies routinely offer late-night "adult entertainment" fare that is soft-core or nudity laden. In the name of education, HBO's *Real Sex* series has aired explicit segments on masturbation techniques and bondage. Some public television affiliates have offered series like Armisted Maupin's *Tales of the City,* a three-part serial on homosexual "bathhouse life" in San Francisco, complete with frontal nudity and foul language.

The growth of the Internet has spawned thousands of web sites that contain pornographic images, many of them accessible to children. *Sex* is the most frequently used search word on the net today, and trading in sexually explicit imagery is now "one of the largest (if not the largest) recreational applications of users of computer networks."[15] Worst of all, perhaps because hard-core sex pictures are readily available elsewhere, "the adult...market seems to be driven largely by a demand for images that can't be found in the average magazine rack: pedophilia (sex with children), hebephilia (youths), and what the researchers call paraphilia—a grab bag of images of bondage, sadomasochism, urination, defecation, and sex acts with a barnyard full of animals."[16]

Recent rulings on the first amendment's application to cyberspace have failed to restrict such fare, making it essential that parents police their children's computer activity and make use of available software that locks out objectionable Internet addresses. One expert has said he would no more leave his child alone to cruise the information superhighway than he would allow him to roam by himself in the seediness of Times Square!

THE ADDICTION OF SEXUAL ABUSE

Many sexually addictive behaviors are clearly exploitative of others. Rape, incest, and child molestation are all-too-common examples. Rape occurs when physical force is used to engage a person in sex against his or her will. Incest is defined as sexual activity between members of a biological family, while child molestation is an adult engaging in sex acts with a dependent child by using physical or emotional force.

While estimates vary widely, it is believed that 25 to 33 percent of all women have at some time in their lives been sexually abused and 10 to 15 percent of all men have suffered sexual abuse.[17] A poll on incest taken a few years ago revealed that about 5 percent of adult women and 2 percent of adult men had sexual experiences with a parent or stepparent of the opposite sex while growing up.[18] Rape, too, is an act of abuse that often occurs between acquaintances, not strangers. The term "date rape" has been coined to describe forced sex in a dating situation. The date rapist has an ego-centric, distorted view of sexuality that causes him to rationalize, *I want sex; I have a right to sex; this woman must, deep down, really want to have sex with me.*

Adult survivors of sexual abuse report that the lingering effects of their experiences are manifested in shame, fear, depression, and other physical and psychological disorders. But perhaps the most damaging effect of this kind of sexual abuse is the victim's resulting inability to trust others. Many victims of abuse report difficulty in establishing committed adult relationships, either because they tend to avoid intimacy altogether, or they tolerate further abuse at the hands of a partner.

Incest victims particularly may feel intense guilt, even though they are innocent of wrongdoing. If the abuse begins at an early age (which it often does), the child has no concept of what is happening, much less that it is wrong. Later the normal tendency to submit to a parent's authority makes him or her hesitant to question or resist the parent's behavior. Typically, the perpetrator of the abuse will use blackmail to secure secrecy: "Don't tell anyone what we did, or terrible things will happen—if anyone even believes you."

Who would harm others through coercive sexual behaviors? Many times they are persons who have been sexually abused themselves. Sexual addiction usually begins in unhealthy families. Sex addicts typically have a very poor self-image which frequently leads to chronic depression. Over 70 percent of the sexual addicts in one survey had considered suicide.[19] Sex addicts use sex to cope with feelings of shame and emotional pain and have an intense need for control. They have four core beliefs about themselves: 1) I am a bad, unworthy person; 2) No one will love me as I am; 3) No one can take care of my needs but me; and 4) Sex is my most important need.[20] These beliefs are manifested in behaviors harmful to themselves and to others.

ESCAPING THE TRAP OF ADDICTION

It is possible to be free from addiction, but the road to wholeness runs through surrender. Escaping addiction, especially sexual addiction, requires that we surrender or submit our will to a higher power—and that higher power is Jesus Christ. We are simply not able to be conquerors on our own. Listen to the apostle Paul—one of the most powerful, charismatic Christians who ever walked the planet—claim his inadequacy to manage his personal demons of addictive behavior: "For the good that I wish, I do not do; but I practice the very evil that I do not wish. But if I am doing the very thing I do not wish, I am no longer the one doing it, but sin which dwells in me. I find then the principle that evil is present in me.... Wretched man that I am! Who will set me free from the body of this death?" (Romans 7:19–21, 24). Then, in the next breath, Paul answers his own question: "Thanks be to God through Jesus Christ our Lord!... There is therefore now no condemnation for those who are in Christ Jesus. For the law of the Spirit of life in Christ Jesus has set you free from the law of sin and of death" (Romans 7:25–8:2).

Author and pastor John Piper, in his excellent book *Future Grace,* says that to successfully conquer lust, we must fight fire with fire: "If we try to fight the fire of lust with prohibitions and threats alone—even the terrible warnings of Jesus—we will fail. We must fight it with *a massive promise of superior happiness* (emphasis mine). We must swallow up the little flicker of lust's pleasure in the conflagration of holy satisfaction.... Our aim is not merely to avoid something erotic, but to gain something excellent."[21] Piper contends (and I heartily agree!) that we fight sin in the sexual area by believing more in the promise of God than in the promise of lust. We must be convinced that the awesome grace that saves us is the same grace that keeps on sustaining us—and that what God will do in our future is every bit as glorious and good as what He has already done in our past!

Quite simply, it is an either/or proposition. Either we believe God is who He says that He is and is able to do what He claims He can do, or we do not. We can't say that we trust Him and continue to cling to our sexual sin. Peaceful coexistence is not an option. Jesus' sacrificial death and resurrection did not give us an excuse to befriend sin, but the power to defeat it. C. S. Lewis spins a remarkable story in *The Great Divorce* about a red lizard that a certain ghost carried on its shoulder. The lizard twitched its tail and whispered beguilingly to the ghost day after day. The ghost urged him to be quiet, but the lizard never heeded.

One day, a bright, shining presence appeared with an offer to rid the ghost of his troublesome baggage, but the ghost refused. He understood that to quiet the beast it would be necessary to kill it, something he was not prepared to do.

Then a series of rationalizations began. Perhaps the lizard need not die; perhaps it could be trained, suppressed, put to sleep, or gotten rid of gradually. The presence insisted that the gradual approach was useless in dealing with such crafty reptiles. It must be all or nothing. It must be the death of the lizard or the defeat of its "host."

Finally, with the ghost's permission, the presence twisted the lizard away from him, flinging it to the ground and breaking its back. With the lizard's death, an amazing thing happened: The ghost became a perfect man, and the lizard became an incredibly beautiful silver and gold stallion, full of beauty and power. The new man leaped astride the great horse, and the two galloped into the morning as one.

Lewis ended his story with these words: "What is a lizard compared with a stallion? Lust is a weak, poor, whimpering, whispering thing compared with that richness and energy of desire which will arise when lust has been killed."

What steps can the sexual addict take to "kill" his particular addiction? He can choose to make of his life a temple, not a trash can. He can seek to cleanse himself. Second Timothy 2:21 says, "Therefore, if a man cleanses himself from these things, he will be a vessel for honor, sanctified, useful to the Master, prepared for every good work." Either a man is clean or he is dirty. If a man decides to "clean up his act," he is on the road to wholeness. But he must choose. The sexual addict must ask himself if his sin has yielded him real, lasting pleasure. If it has, he can choose to wear its chains again, *but if it has not,* he should set it aside.

Then what? Timothy says "flee from youthful lusts" (2 Timothy 2:22). That means getting off the wrong track and onto the right track. Then, "pursue righteousness, faith, love and peace" (2 Timothy

2:22). It is not enough to reject what is filthy. We must embrace what is good and clean and right. Where in this world do we find righteousness, faith, love, and peace? I know only one true source. His name is Jesus. Make Him your target. Aim at Him. He can supernaturally change you, change your appetite, and change the direction of the cycle that led you into a captive lifestyle. Make Him your target. He'll give you the power to make the change.

Finally, pursue Him and the qualities of righteousness, faith, love, and peace, with "those who call on the Lord from a pure heart." In other words, get on the right team. Identify yourself with God's people. Surround yourself with godly friends. The most saintly disciple who ever lived would not stand a chance surrounded twenty-four hours a day, seven days a week, by godless people. Choose the right team.

If you are desperately aware that you need deliverance from addiction today, hear this: You cannot do it alone. Your old man, your sin nature, simply will not let you. It is like the dragon that will not surrender; it is constantly at war with the law of God in your inner man. There is a battle going on, and you—your body, your mind, your soul—are the battleground! That is why it takes the supernatural Christ to come into your life and face that dragon with you, head-on. He is the dragon slayer. He defeated sin and death. He can defeat addiction. God's Word promises it is so.

And why is it so? Because Jesus swallowed up the power of sin forever on a garbage dump of a hill called Golgotha. With His sacrificial death He became our "garbage man." He willingly takes the trash out of your life and my life and covers it with His blood, transforming what was once a trash heap into a temple.

So ask Him. He'll do it for you. It's what He was born to do.

You Can Go Home Again

I t's 12:00 A.M. on the West Coast, an hour when most of the country is asleep. In a brightly lit, cramped studio at a talk-radio station thousands of miles away, the calls are coming in. The topic making the phones ring is sex.

"San Bernardino, you're on the air. Talk to me."

"Yeah, man, this is Cal. I was calling because I have different questions. The thing is, I feel, like, incomplete without someone in my life. Even if I did have someone, eventually, within a few months or so, I would want to have a close, intimate relationship with that person. You know what I mean?"

"I think so, but let me make sure. How do *you* define intimate, Cal?"

"Hmmm...well..."

"You mean you want to have sex, right?"

"Uh...right."

"So are you saying you equate sex with intimacy?"

"Yeah. I guess so. That's part of it."

"Well, Cal, there *is* a difference...and you need to know that. You had another question?"

"OK. My second question is, why do I feel incomplete without a relationship? Why is it so hard to be alone?"

"It's hard to be alone because you and I were made for relationship, Cal. The problem is, we don't realize that the primary relationship we need is not with another person. It's much bigger than that. And anything or anyone we expect to fill all of our relational needs is ultimately going to disappoint us. If we're honest, most of us would have to say that we're looking for *the* perfect love. And there is only one perfect, capital-L Lover."

On the Santa Monica freeway, a woman dials her car phone. She is leaving a club alone, but she had hoped to find someone there to spend the next few hours with—someone who might make her feel attractive and desirable and who could perhaps temporarily ease her loneliness.

"This is Night Line. Is the caller there?"

"Hi. This is Marci."

"Marci, what's on your mind tonight?"

"Well, I'm just calling to say that I'm not sure about all that 'perfect love' stuff you're talking about. I'm a lesbian, see, and I have sex with a lot of different partners. I don't think there's anything wrong with it, either. I'm not sure one person can meet all my needs. In fact, I'm studying psychology, and all of my instructors say serial monogamy is the norm these days."

"Serial monogamy…is that like 'love the one you're with'?"

"That's right."

"So, Marci, let me ask you a question: are you in a committed relationship?"

"Uh, no, I'm not."

"But you're happy with your situation? You're saying you have a great love life and that being with one person would be too limiting for you?"

"Well, I mean, not *totally* happy. I guess what I don't really feel like I'm getting is intimacy. But how do you get that?"

"Boy—what a great question, Marci. We're coming up on a break, but stay on the line, and I'll come right back to you, OK?"

Half an hour later, the phones in the studio are still lit and blinking. The host is nursing a cup of reheated coffee and pulls on his headphones as he takes one more sip. Music comes up, then fades. On the other side of a glass wall, the producer holds up her hand to give him his cue.

"Good morning, L. A.! You're on the air."

"Yeah, this is Max, and I just had my girlfriend leave because she found out I have herpes. I was real careful and stuff, and she hasn't got it, but now I'm wondering if I'm ever going to find somebody who will just accept me the way I am. I mean, if you tell people right off, that's gonna scare 'em away…but if you wait and they find out after you have sex, then they're all mad, and they don't want you anymore."

"Max, do you think your girlfriend had a reason to be angry?"

"Yeah, I suppose. But I didn't mean to hurt her. I would have told her later."

"How much later?"

"Well, you know, when I was more sure of her."

"Max, I *do* think you have to tell someone that you're sleeping with that you have a sexually transmitted disease. But I also think you should consider how you got that disease and whether or not the lifestyle you've been living is ever going to bring you the kind of love you're looking for. Do you hear what I'm saying?"

Maybe. But Max hangs up before he can hear any more. There is another caller waiting.

"Hello…this is Night Line. Who am I talking to?"

"Renee."

"Renee…we're glad to hear from you. Do you have a question?"

"No, I really have more of a comment…is that OK?"

"Sure. Fire away."

"I just wanted to say that I think maybe sex really was meant just for marriage."

"Whoa—Renee! You know some folks are going to think that's pretty radical! What makes you say such a thing?"

"I…I was molested a long time ago, and what sex outside of marriage does is violate your soul. I've been married for twenty-five years now to a man I think is faithful, and most of the time I'm very happy with him, but there are things I still struggle with that are related to what happened in the past. Because of that, you wind up with things in your life that are not good. Like, I have a real hard time with trust. I've tried so hard to trust my husband, but it's not easy. I mean, I wish all that other stuff had never happened, but I just can't seem to forget it. It won't go away."[1]

And so it goes. Caller after caller, voice after voice, filled with uncertainty, anger, pain, regret, defiance. Their stories are different. But their lives have one single common denominator: They are unsatisfied with sex because it has not delivered what it seemed to promise. It has not brought them the love and intimacy they are longing for. It has not made them feel complete.

They live in what could be called the sexual "far country." They are a long way from the warmth and security of home, and they know it. But they are by no means alone. This handful of callers on a random night represents countless men and women who have sold themselves short in the area of sex. They are not statistics. They are real people who are missing the joy, peace, fulfillment, and wholeness that God intended us to experience.

What they long for most of all is intimacy: being deeply known, understood, and loved by another. Augustine said the heart of man is restless until it finds its rest in God. The total intimacy we seek from others will be found only in Him, but we continue, like stubborn children, to try to force the square peg of sex into the round hole in our hearts that God Himself desires to fill. "God is love," the apostle John said, but we have reversed the order of that truth in our minds and behave as if "love is god."

Perhaps it was the title of this book, *Pure Sex,* that caused you to pick it up and begin to read. Whatever prompted you, I trust you have been challenged to consider the truth about sex from the Author of love. He has a higher way, a better way for living—and His way works! He has placed His boundaries around the gift of sex, yes—but they are meant to be protective, not restrictive. By living within them, we can experience the sheer delight of pure sex, sex that is free from manipulation and fear and which mirrors His pure and perfect love for us.

I am very aware that many who are reading this have not prac-
ticed the principles put forth in *Pure Sex*. Perhaps you are involved
in a relationship that you know is not right, or you feel trapped in
an addictive behavior or lifestyle that is draining the joy, the freedom, even the very *life* from you. Or perhaps it is your past that
continues to haunt you, even though you have managed to hide the
details of your particular indiscretion. If so, I have good news: God
is in the salvaging business. To salvage something is to rescue it from
destruction and *to restore it to the purpose for which it was originally
intended.*

You and I were originally intended to have unbroken fellowship
with God and to receive His perfect, unconditional love. He intended
that we love Him in return and worship Him for who He is. "We
love, because He first loved us" (1 John 4:19). If you do not take
another thing from this book, remember this: There is nothing you
have done or ever dreamed of doing that would keep God from loving you and drawing you to Himself. Nothing! All He asks is that you
turn to Him. Right now, He has His eyes on you and is ready to run
in your direction. He is waiting for you to turn and call Him "Father."

THE FATHER WHO WAITS

The greatest storyteller who ever lived illustrated it this way:

"There was once a man who had two sons. The younger said
to his father, 'Father, I want right now what's coming to me.'

"So the father divided the property between them. It
wasn't long before the younger son packed his bags and left
for a distant country. There, undisciplined and dissipated, he
wasted everything he had. After he had gone through all his
money, there was a bad famine all through that country and
he began to hurt. He signed on with a citizen there who
assigned him to his fields to slop the pigs. He was so hungry
he would have eaten the corncobs in the pig slop, but no
one would give him any.

"That brought him to his senses. He said, 'All those
farmhands working for my father sit down to three meals a

day, and here I am starving to death. I'm going back to my father. I'll say to him, "Father, I've sinned against God, I've sinned before you; I don't deserve to be called your son. Take me on as a hired hand."' He got right up and went home to his father.

"When he was still a long way off, his father saw him. His heart pounding, he ran out, embraced him, and kissed him. The son started his speech: 'Father, I've sinned against God, I've sinned before you; I don't deserve to be called your son ever again.'

"But the father wasn't listening. He was calling to the servants, 'Quick. Bring a clean set of clothes and dress him. Put the family ring on his finger and sandals on his feet. Then get a grain-fed heifer and roast it. We're going to feast! We're going to have a wonderful time! My son is here—given up for dead and now alive! Given up for lost and now found!' And they began to have a wonderful time.

"All this time his older son was out in the field. When the day's work was done he came in. As he approached the house, he heard the music and dancing. Calling over one of the houseboys, he asked what was going on. He told him, 'Your brother came home. Your father has ordered a feast—barbecued beef!—because he has him home safe and sound.'

"The older brother stalked off in an angry sulk and refused to join in. His father came out and tried to talk to him, but he wouldn't listen. The son said, 'Look how many years I've stayed here serving you, never giving you one moment of grief, but have you ever thrown a party for me and my friends? Then this son of yours who has thrown away your money on whores shows up and you go all out with a feast!'

"His father said, 'Son, you don't understand. You're with me all the time, and everything that is mine is yours—but this is a wonderful time, and we had to celebrate. This brother of yours was dead, and he's alive! He was lost, and he's found!' "[2]

Perhaps you recognize this as the parable of the prodigal son, told by Jesus to His disciples. The younger son in the story was a long way from home. He had lost everything in the distant country and thought perhaps he was too far gone to ever return to his father's house. We all have been there. Henri Nouwen writes, "Over and over again I have left home. I have fled from the hands of blessing and run off to faraway places searching for love! This is the great tragedy of my life and the lives of so many I meet on my journey. Somehow I have become deaf to the voice that calls me the Beloved, have left the only place where I can hear that voice, and have gone off desperately hoping that I would find somewhere else what I could no longer find at home."[3] Each of us becomes the prodigal son every time we search for unconditional love where it cannot be found.

But the prodigal in this story finally realized he was hungry. Lost. And alone. So he swallowed what little pride he had left and started home. That turning homeward is where the real drama begins for every child of God who has strayed. Because when a son turns, his father runs. Nowhere else in all of the Bible do we see God run, yet He runs—and is running still—toward every prodigal who finally heads for home.

The words of this story assure us that we can never sink so low that God is not there. You *can* go home again. You *can* be caught up in the Father's embrace and enjoy the pure love of God. You *can* abandon the sexual far country and know the thrill of pure sex once again, once and for all.

And if you are the older brother in this story, if you have never left home for the far country or have already returned—rejoice! Don't consider yourself somehow better than those who have been starving in the far country and are desperately looking to fill their hunger. Don't view the returning sexual prodigal with scorn or envy or bitterness. Remember that you have been blessed with everything that is God's, so thank Him for the privilege of being in His presence for so long.

Do not be resentful; instead be grateful. "Resentment and gratitude cannot coexist, since resentment blocks the perception and experience of life as a gift. My resentment tells me that I don't receive what I deserve. It always manifests itself in envy. Gratitude, however, goes beyond the 'mine' and 'thine' and claims the truth that all of life is a pure gift. The discipline of gratitude is the explicit effort to acknowledge that all I am and have is given to me as a gift of love, a gift to be celebrated with joy."[4]

Prodigal or older brother, sink down deep in the pure love of God and let Him fill the hole in your heart. Then, and *only* then, will you be able to enjoy the true, unselfish, pure love that is the source of pure sex.

Turn to Him.

Wait on Him.

Follow Him.

Cling to Him.

His way works—and it is the only way out of the far country and home to fulfillment.

Study Guide

CHAPTER ONE

Sex

1. The author says that *sex* is the most frequently used search word on the Internet.

    a. How does this fact make you feel? Explain.

    b. What do you think this says about the state of our culture?

2. The author says that the church has been largely silent about sex.

    a. Do you agree? Why or why not?

    b. What have you learned about sex from the church? Has your experience been positive or negative? Explain.

3. The author says that the Bible should be a Christian's final authority on sex.

    a. Why does he say this?

    b. As you begin this study, what do you believe the Bible says about sex?

    c. Read 2 Timothy 3:16–17. What does this text tell us about the Bible? What does this imply about its perspective on sex?

4. Do you agree that the only proper framework for sexual intercourse is a total, intimate, lifetime commitment of marriage? Why or why not?

5. The author writes that sex thrives in an atmosphere of committed love.

   a. What does he mean by "an atmosphere of committed love"? How is this created?

   b. How does such an atmosphere encourage sex to "thrive"?

6. Why is sex "one of the most intimate, life-altering, profound, and deeply spiritual experiences available to man"? Has this been true in your own experience? Explain.

7. The author says pleasure is just as valid a reason for the divine creation of sex as is procreation.

   a. Why does he say this? What rationale does he give for his statement?

   b. Do you agree with him? Why or why not?

8. There are two equal errors people make about sex:

   They see sex as evil;

   They make it an idol.

a. Why do some people see sex as evil? Is it? Explain.

b. In what way do some people make sex into an idol? Do you know anyone who has done so? If so, explain.

9. There may be at least two reasons for feeling guilty about sex:

The person has actually sinned and therefore feels guilt;

The person is unsure about what's really right or wrong.

In the following verses, what sexual activities does the Bible call sin?

a. 1 Corinthians 6:18; 7:2–5; Hebrews 13:4

b. Leviticus 18:6–18

c. Romans 1:26–27; 1 Corinthians 6:9

d. Exodus 22:19; Leviticus 20:13–16

e. Matthew 5:27–28

f. 1 Corinthians 13:4–7; Philippians 2:3–4

10. How would you answer the questions on page 28?

11. There are at least four primary biblical truths to keep in mind about sex:

    a. Sex was God's idea—Read Genesis 2. What do you learn about God's plan here?

    b. Human sexuality is unique—Read Genesis 2:19–20. How is human sexuality different from that of animals?

    c. Sexual intercourse involves every aspect of our being—Read Genesis 2:23. In what way does sex involve every aspect of our being?

    d. Sex requires boundaries—Read Genesis 2:24–25. What boundaries are set here? Why these boundaries? What happens when they are crossed? Explain.

CHAPTER TWO

The State of the Union

1. If a wealthy person were to offer you a million dollars for a "one-night stand," would you consider the proposal? Explain. How about for ten million dollars? One billion?

2. When someone commits adultery and tells his or her mate, "It didn't mean anything," why does the offended party often feel insulted? Why does it "mean something" to that person?

3. In what way is marriage a "sacred covenant"? Why is breaking this covenant so serious?

4. Read 1 Corinthians 6:16. In what way is sexual intercourse a "soul-uniting act"? How is this significant?

5. The author outlines what he calls "the anatomy of an affair." Explain each of the following steps, and take inventory whether you are at risk through any of these steps:

   a. A seemingly inconsequential rift

   b. An unrealized dream

   c. Worldly success

   d. Loss of a significant relationship

e. Disengagement from the daily grind

6. The author lists three categories of persons who cheat on their mate. Describe in your own words what these categories mean, and consider whether you are in danger of falling into any of the three:

a. Those with unsatisfied appetites

b. Adolescent adults

c. Those with unresolved conflict

If you recognize yourself in any of these categories, what are you going to do about it? What steps can you take now to avoid adultery and strengthen your marriage?

7. Read Romans 6:23. How does this verse agree with the author's warning that adulterers "are not safe" and that adultery "will take the very heart out of your life"?

8. Read John 4:1–42 and 8:1–11. How do these passages show that adultery is not the unpardonable sin and that God forgives those who repent?

9. The author lists four key elements in affair-proofing your marriage:

a. Admit the possibility.

(1) Why is it important to admit the possibility that you could engage in an affair?

(2) Look at the temptations listed on pages 47–48. How are you doing in these areas?

(3) Read 1 Corinthians 10:12. How does this verse relate to the author's suggestion?

b. Expect temptation.

(1) Why should you expect temptation?

(2) What might happen if you're not expecting temptation? Explain.

c. Do not be afraid of temptation.

(1) Does temptation ever frighten you? Why or why not?

(2) Read 1 Corinthians 10:13. Why does this verse encourage us to remain unfearful of temptation? Are you taking advantage of its truth? Explain.

d. Guard your thought life.

(1) Do you monitor and "screen" your thought life? Explain.

(2) Read 2 Corinthians 10:5 and James 1:15. What do these verses tell us to do about our thought life? How can we comply with these commands?

(3) Read Philippians 4:8. List the kinds of things this verse tells us to think about, then name at least five specific examples of each kind. Do you think this way? Explain.

10. The author lists seven components of a "marital security system." To what does each one refer? Does it exist in your own marriage? If not, how can you "install" that component?

a. Be controlled by the love of God.

b. Be wise in the fear of God.

(1) Read Psalm 111:10. What does this verse tell us about the fear of God? How does this relate to marriage?

(2) Read Hebrews 10:26–31. How does this passage relate to the fear of God? How does it relate to your marriage?

c. Be certain of the judgment of God.

(1) Read Hebrews 9:27. According to this verse, how certain is the judgment of God?

(2) How does this relate to marriage? (See also 1 Thessalonians 4:3–6.)

d. Be identified with the cause of God.

e. Be accountable to the people of God.

f. Be your spouse's best option.

g. Be aware of the deception of Satan.

   (1) Review the satanic myths the author lists on pages 54
       and 55. To which of these myths might you be most
       susceptible?

   (2) How can you guard yourself against them?

11. How can you choose, right now, to love your mate? Will you do
    so? Take some time to ask God to help your marriage grow
    strong and avoid the awful destruction caused by adultery.

CHAPTER THREE

A Table for Two

1. One study found that out of 2,000 observed cultures, only 55 blurred gender distinctions—and these all quickly died out.

   a. What is significant about this finding?

   b. How would you categorize our own culture: with the 1,945 cultures who maintained gender distinctions, or with the 55 that blurred them? Explain.

   c. Describe what you consider to be a "real man" and a "real woman." How are they different? In what ways are they the same?

2. The author says that "women are angry" today about the way they are treated by men.

   a. Do you agree with this statement? Explain.

   b. If you are a woman, are you angry about this issue? Explain.

   c. If you are a man, do you think women have a right to be angry about this issue? Explain.

3. The author claims that the number one marriage problem today is ungodly men.

a. What do you think he means by this? Do you agree? Explain.

b. How would you describe a godly man? How would you describe an ungodly man?

c. How might an ungodly man create problems in a marriage that a godly man might avoid? Describe a few examples.

4. The author names and describes four kinds of destructive husbands:

a. Dictator—What are the characteristics of this type of husband? How does he create problems in marriage?

b. Powder puff—What television character does the author use to illustrate this type of husband? What is this man's primary problem? Is he more or less common than the Dictator?

c. Playboy—What is the main problem with this type of husband? What kind of problems does this create in marriage?

d. Driven husband—What is the main problem with this man? Why does the author say his problem is the "most easily camouflaged" of all those he discusses?

e. If you are a husband, which of these descriptions most resembles you? What do you need to do to become a more godly spouse?

5. The author names four roles that must be included in the "job description of a good husband":

  a. Provider—Read 1 Timothy 5:8. How does this describe a provider? How does it show his importance? What things are most important to provide?

  b. Teacher—Read Deuteronomy 4:9–10; 6:4–9. Who is directed to teach in these passages? What is he to teach? To whom? For what purpose?

  c. Leader—Read Ephesians 5:22–23 and Genesis 3:9. In what way is the husband the leader of the home? What does this leadership look like? What does it *not* look like? How did Adam err in his leadership? What were the consequences? How can his story help us today?

  d. Lover—Read Ephesians 5:25–28. What great example is given husbands in this text? Does this surprise you? Explain. How does this text instruct husbands to love their wives? How can this be carried out practically in day-to-day living?

6. The author mentions two of a wife's basic needs:

  a. Nonsexual affection—How is this defined? What does it entail? What does it not entail? Why is it important? If you are a husband, how well are you meeting this need?

  b. Open communication—How is this defined? How is it achieved? What does it produce? What are the consequences when it's lacking? If you are a husband, how well are you meeting this need?

7. Complete the following "Equation for intimacy": 1 + 2 = _____. What does this mean? Why is it so critical in marriage? How well does this equation function in your own marriage? Explain.

8. As a couple, read through the Song of Solomon (it's only eight chapters long). What do you learn of sexual intimacy in this book? How is it portrayed? In what ways can the example of Solomon and the Shulammite energize your own love life?

9. The author names four elements critical for allowing sexual intimacy to develop:

    a. Time

        1. Why is *slow* the operative word?

        2. How much time is enough?

    b. Timing

       Fill in the blanks:

        1. Men are turned on by s_____t; women, by s_____d.

        2. What does the phrase "no leftovers" mean to you? Why is it important?

    c. Timely communication

    (1) How can communication be "timely"? How can it reflect bad timing?

    (2) What difference can this make?

  d. Time away

    (1) Why is it important to take take away? How do you do this? When was the last time you took time away?

    (2) Read the Song of Solomon 7:11–12. How did this couple take time away?

10. If the author is right that sex is a "reliable barometer" of your marital relationship, what is that barometer saying right now? Do you like what it says? If not, what will you do to make a change?

CHAPTER FOUR

A Table for Two

1. The author says women are "programmed" to "respect," "respond," and "nurture."

   a. What does it mean for a wife to respect her husband? How can this be shown? How can this be violated?

   b. What does it mean for a wife to respond to her husband? What might this include in a practical sense?

   c. What does it mean for a wife to nurture her marriage? What are some good ways to nurture a marriage? What are some ways that don't nurture a marriage?

2. The author mentions four kinds of destructive wives:

   a. Domineering wife—What characterizes this kind of wife? What is her main problem?

   b. Doormat wife—What television character does the author use to illustrate this kind of wife? How is she appropriate? What is her main problem?

   c. Roller coaster wife—On what basis does the roller coaster wife operate? What's the problem with this?

   d. Independent wife—How does an independent wife operate? What is the problem with this?

e. If you are a wife, which of these four types do you most resemble? What would it take for you to change for the better?

3. The author says the "job description" of a good wife includes four elements:

a. She loves and fears God.

(1) What does it mean, practically, to love God?

(2) What does it mean to fear God? How does this fit with loving Him?

(3) Read Proverbs 31:30. How does this verse picture loving and fearing God?

b. She is a helper to her husband.

(1) Read Genesis 2:18, 20–22. What reason is given here for Eve's creation? How is this significant?

(2) Read Proverbs 31:10–11, 13–18. How was this wife a helper to her husband?

c. She honors her husband.

(1) What does it look like when a wife honors her husband?

(2) Read Ephesians 5:33. What is commanded in the second half of this verse? How is this command to be obeyed?

d. She is her husband's best friend and lover.

   (1) Read Song of Solomon 5:16. What kind of friend and lover is described here?

   (2) How can this woman be an example for us today?

4. A husband has two basic needs in marriage: "acceptance and appreciation," and "intimate connection."

   a. What are some practical ways for a wife to show her husband acceptance? How can she show her appreciation for him?

   b. What does the author mean by "intimate connection"? How can this effectively be made?

   c. If you are a wife, how well do you think you are meeting these two major needs of your husband? Explain.

5. The author lists four attitudes of a sexually responsive wife:

   a. A positive attitude

      (1) What are some ways to develop and show a positive attitude? What are some things to avoid?

      (2) Read the Song of Solomon 1:2–4. How did the Shulammite show a positive attitude? What happened when she did so?

b. A healthy self-image

    (1) Name some elements of a healthy self-image. How can these be developed? Name some things that destroy a healthy self-image. How can these be avoided?

    (2) Read the Song of Solomon 1:5. How did the Shulammite feel about herself? How did this help her to be a good wife?

c. Uninhibited initiative

    (1) When should a wife take the initiative? How can she effectively do so?

    (2) Read the Song of Solomon 2:3–6; 7:1–4. How did the Shulammite take the initiative? What happened as a result?

d. Enthusiastic availability

    (1) How can a wife show enthusiastic availability? What is the opposite of this?

    (2) Read 1 Corinthians 7:3. What does this text teach about availability? How is it shown?

CHAPTER FIVE

Pure Lovemaking

1. What does the author mean by the "duality of body and spirit"? Is this idea in the Bible? What difference does it make?

2. There are at least three primary words in Greek used for the idea of love. Describe each one and tell how they differ from one another:

   a. *agape*

   b. *eros*

   c. *philos*

Which of these words best describes your own love life? Explain.

3. The author says *agape* love is essential.

   a. What does he mean by this? Why is it essential?

   b. Read 1 Corinthians 13:1–3. How does this passage show the essential character of *agape* love? Is this kind of love expressed in your own marriage? Explain.

4. The author lists twelve characteristics of *agape* love that must be expressed in marriage. For each characteristic listed:
   a. give a working definition of the term;
   b. describe how it is being expressed in your marriage;

c. suggest practical ways of increasing its expression...then follow through!

(1) Is patient

(2) Is kind

(3) Does not envy

(4) Is not boastful or proud

(5) Is not rude

(6) Is not easily angered

(7) Does not rejoice in iniquity

(8) Bears all things

(9) Believes all things

(10) Hopes all things

(11) Perseveres

(12) Endures

CHAPTER SIX

"Where Did I Come From?"

1. What kind of sexual information have your children already received from sources outside the home? Have you been pleased with this? Explain.

2. The author lists five guidelines for teaching your children about sex:

   a. Know your goal.

      (1) What is your own goal in teaching your kids about sex?

      (2) Read Proverbs 7:4. What goal is named here?

      (3) The author says a Christian world-view features at least four elements:

      There is a God;

      God created the world;

      God loves us and has a plan for us;

      It is possible to know God through Jesus.

How are you teaching your kids about all four of these elements? What are you doing right? How might you do better?

b. Start early and keep at it.

    (1) How early are you starting to teach your kids the basics of sex?

    (2) Have you let setbacks keep you from continuing? Explain.

c. Model what you teach.

    (1) What does your own sexual practice teach your kids?

    (2) Would you want them to emulate you? Explain.

d. Tell it like it is.

    (1) How honest are you with your kids on this topic? Does it embarrass you? Explain.

    (2) Read Proverbs 7. How does this chapter demonstrate honesty in teaching a son about sex? What principles can you glean from Solomon's method?

e. Tell it like it ought to be.

    (1) How ought it to be? Why?

    (2) What plan do you have in place to show your kids how it ought to be? Describe it.

3. The author suggests the kinds of sexual information that are appropriate to share with children at four stages of maturity. Take inventory of your teaching methods according to this suggested schedule, and ask how you're doing at each relevant level. If you are not at a particular stage yet, discuss how you will prepare for it:

a. Ages 0–5

    (1) Use correct terminology.

    (2) Allow all questions.

b. Ages 6–9

    (1) Give basic facts regarding sexual intercourse and human reproduction.

c. Ages 10–13

    (1) Give more detail about sexual intercourse.

    (2) Discuss puberty.

    (3) Discuss abortion.

    (4) Talk about stages of growth.

    (5) Warn about the dangers of sexual abuse and sexual predators.

d. Ages 14–18

(1) Set guidelines for dating.

(2) Discuss kissing, petting, sexual experimentation.

4. The author mentions three things held in common by teens who decide to wait for sex until marriage:

a. A sense of self as a special individual—How are you (or will you be) developing this trait in your children? What specifically will you do? What will you avoid?

b. A reverence for God and His principles—How are you (or will you be) developing this trait in your children? How will you help them become God's friend?

c. Prizing the worth of others—How are you (or will you be) teaching your children to prize others?

CHAPTER SEVEN

"But We Love Each Other!"

1. Recall the story of the woman in the movie who boasted about having thirty-three lovers. Do you think this is common? Explain. How do you react to this? Explain.

2. How does our culture view unmarried sex as an entitlement? Give a few examples in your own observation.

3. Peter Kreeft writes that "true love includes awe." What does he mean by this? Do you agree? Why or why not?

4. The author lists three kinds of uncommitted sex:

   a. "So what?" sex—recreational

      (1) Describe this kind of sex. What is wrong with it?

      (2) How does this category highlight the difference between "intent" and "action"?

   b. "Who knows?" sex—experimental

      (1) Describe this kind of sex. What is wrong with it?

      (2) In what way do couples who engage in "who knows?" sex do so because they think it *might* lead to commitment? What is wrong with this thinking?

c. "Oh, well" sex—preceremonial

(1) What's wrong with "Oh, well" sex?

(2) How can one prevent it from happening?

5. In what way is unmarried sex second-rate? Why do you think many people don't see it this way?

6. The Bible gives three general prohibitions regarding sexual activity. According to the following verses, what are they, and why do they exist?

a. _____ (see Exodus 20:14; Hebrews 13:4)

b. _____ (see 1 Corinthians 6:13–20; 1 Thessalonians 4:3–8)

c. _____ (see Matthew 5:27–30; 1 Corinthians 6:9–11)

7. Beyond the physical and emotional price of uncommitted sex, there is a spiritual price to pay. Read Psalm 51:1–4, 9–11; 66:18. What are some of these spiritual costs? Are they ever worth it? Explain.

8. Is it wise to see how "close to the edge" one can get to sexual temptation without falling off the cliff? Explain. What are the dangers? Why is the question, "What's wrong with it?" a bad place to begin?

9. The author warns singles not to tempt members of the opposite sex to a point of frustration. What does this mean? How does one avoid this?

10. Read 2 Timothy 2:22. What counsel does this verse give singles about their dating lives?

11. The author describes three stages of physical involvement prior to intercourse:

Stage one: kissing, hugging, holding hands

Stage two: light petting

Stage three: heavy petting

What is meant by each stage? Which stage(s) are OK for unmarried couples to engage in? Why?

12. Why does the author say that unmarried sex is uncommitted sex? Do you agree? Explain.

CHAPTER EIGHT

Just Say Yes!

1. The author says every person has a deep desire for connection and the transcendent.

    a. What does he mean? Do you notice this in your own life? Explain.

    b. How do you achieve connection in your life? Are you satisfied with this? Explain.

2. Tim Stafford writes, "By not depriving single people of bad sex, we end up depriving them of good sex."

    a. What does he mean by this? Do you agree? Why or why not?

    b. In Stafford's view, what is good sex? How is it achieved?

3. How can single people say yes to a higher love?

4. The author notes four keys to relational intimacy:

    a. Time

        (1) How is time a key to relational intimacy? How can cutting short on time short-circuit a relationship?

(2) In your opinion, how much time is enough to build a solid relationship? Explain.

b. Talk

(1) What kind of talk is critical? Why is it hard to achieve? Why is it essential? How much do you talk with your own significant other?

(2) Read the Song of Solomon 1:9–10; 2:3–4; 4:1, 9, 15; 5:16. What kind of talk do you notice here? What is significant about it? What can you learn from it?

c. Truth

(1) What kind of truth is essential to building a strong relationship? How can the lack of it destroy a relationship? Discuss any examples of the latter you know of.

(2) Read Ephesians 4:15 and 1 John 3:18. How should the truth of these verses affect our relationships? Do we allow them to? Explain.

d. Touch

(1) What kind of touch is appropriate between unmarried couples? What is inappropriate? Why?

(2) How does appropriate touch help build godly intimacy? Does it in your own relationship(s)? Explain.

5. How does the author compare the development of relational intimacy to a game of basketball? How do "rules" foster such intimacy? How does their absence prevent it?

6. What is God's "higher call" as outlined in 2 Timothy 2:22? Are you following this higher call? Explain.

7. What is God's "higher call" as outlined in 1 Corinthians 6:19–20? Are you following this higher call? Explain.

8. If you've already "blown it" in this area, is there hope for healing? If so, how may it be found?

9. Read 1 John 1:9. How does this verse relate to the single and sex? What does it instruct? What does it promise?

10. You have a choice about how you will seek fulfillment in the area of relational intimacy. What are you choosing? Explain.

CHAPTER NINE

Gay Sex

1. How does the media in your town or city portray homosexuality? As an alternate lifestyle? As a legitimate minority?

2. What is your opinion about homosexuality? Do you think it is right or wrong? Explain.

3. Read the following texts: Genesis 19:1–20; Exodus 20:3; Leviticus 18:22; 20:13; Judges 19:1–25; Romans 1:24–27; 1 Corinthians 6:9–11; 1 Timothy 1:9–11.

   a. What do these texts say about the homosexual practice?

   b. What is God's opinion about this practice?

4. The author discusses the following six myths about homosexuality that are actively propagated in the media and culture today. Have you heard each of these myths? What is your own reaction to them?

   a. Homosexuality is a normal, comfortable, healthy, even desirable lifestyle. (The truth: The median age of death for active homosexual men is thirty-eight; for women, forty-five.)

   b. Old Masters and Johnson studies continue to be quoted today which say that fully one-tenth of the population is homosexual. (The truth: A more recent Chicago study says only 2.8 percent of the male population and 1.4 percent of the female population are active homosexuals.)

c. The only people opposed to homosexual practice either suffer from homophobia or hatred. (The truth: There are ample biblical grounds for opposing homosexuality that have nothing to do with homophobia or hatred.)

d. Homosexuality is genetic and is inherited. (The truth: Recent studies refute old claims that homosexuality is inherited; its genesis is uncertain, but early home life seems to be a large factor.)

e. If one has homosexual desires, they must be acted upon. (The truth: Human beings have all kinds of sinful desires that can and must be refused; the Holy Spirit empowers believers to resist sin of all kinds.)

f. Homosexuality is an immutable fact of life; one cannot change. (The truth: There are many men and women who formerly acted out their homosexual urges who are now either in monogamous, loving, heterosexual relationships, or are celibate.)

5. Recall the stories of Odysseus and Orpheus.

a. How did Odysseus resist the sirens' song? How did Orpheus resist the sirens' song?

b. Who would you say was the most successful?

c. How can a comparison of these two ancient stories help us to pursue godliness today?

CHAPTER TEN

Sexual Chaos

1. The Bible does not use the word *addiction,* but it does use the word *slavery* to describe the same thing.

   a. Read John 8:34. What does Jesus say sin does to us? In what way is it an addiction?

   b. Read Romans 7:14. How does this verse picture sin? How is this like an addiction?

   c. Read Romans 6:6–7. How does this verse tell us we can be free of our addiction to sin?

2. The author uses the Old Testament figure Samson as an example of a sexual addict and pictures his road to personal downfall like this:

   a. Fantasy: "She looks good to me."

      (1) How does sexual addiction always begin with fantasy? How can it be cut off right at the start?

      (2) Read Philippians 4:8. How does this text tell us to deal with sexual fantasy? With what are we to replace it?

   b. Ritualization: cruising strange places

(1) Samson "cruised" strange places looking at forbidden women. How was this his ritual before engaging in forbidden sex?

(2) Are there any such rituals in your own life? If so, what are you going to do about them?

c. Realization: acting out the fantasy

(1) Why is it true that when people act out their fantasy, they are saying to God, "You cannot or will not meet my deepest longings, so I'll do it on my own"?

(2) What does it mean that abstinence is not the cure, merely the precondition, to recovering from sexual addiction?

d. Paralysis: no longer a choice

(1) Have you ever felt in your sexual life that you didn't have a choice about what you were about to do? If so, you may be a victim of paralysis.

(2) What will you do about it?

e. Desensitization: no longer a conscience

(1) Read Romans 1:24–28. How does this passage describe the progression to desensitization?

(2) What is the conclusion of this slide?

3. No one has to remain a slave to sexual addictions. The author suggests several steps to freedom:

    a. Surrender to God.

        (1) How does one surrender to God? What does this entail?

        (2) Read Romans 7:19, 24–8:2. What do these verses say about surrendering to God? What is the result?

    b. Flee and pursue.

        (1) Read 2 Timothy 2:22. What are we to flee? What are we to pursue?

        (2) What is the goal of this instruction?

    c. Surround yourself with godly friends.

        (1) What does a godly friend look like? How do you find such friends?

        (2) Read 1 Corinthians 15:33. What does this verse say about friends?

        (3) Read Hebrews 10:24–25. What does this verse say that godly friends do for each other? Do you have such friends?

4. The author says, "You can go home again."

    a. What does he mean by this? How can you "go home" again?

    b. Read 1 John 1:7, 9. How do these verses point the way back home?

5. Compare 1 Corinthians 5:1–13 with 2 Corinthians 2:5–11.

    a. What was the young man's sin in 1 Corinthians?

    b. How did Paul instruct the church to deal with this sin? Does this seem harsh to you? Explain. Why do you think Paul so instructed the church?

    c. What happened by 2 Corinthians 2:5–11 to change the apostle's mind?

    d. How is this an example that "you can go home again"?

$\mathscr{N}otes$

INTRODUCTION

1. Peter Kreeft, *Everything You Always Wanted to Know about Heaven* (San Francisco: Ignatius Press, 1990), 117.

2. Richard Foster, *Money, Sex & Power: The Challenge of the Disciplined Life* (San Francisco: Harper & Row, 1985), 92.

3. C. S. Lewis, *Mere Christianity* (1943; reprint, New York: Touchstone, Simon & Schuster, 1996), 91.

4. Bill Hybels, *Tender Love* (Chicago: Moody Press, 1993), 51.

CHAPTER ONE: SEX

1. John Gray, *Mars and Venus in the Bedroom* (New York: HarperCollins Publishers, 1995), 20.

2. "The Joy of What?" *Wall Street Journal*, 12 December 1995.

3. As quoted by Philip Yancey in *Christianity Today*.

4. C. S. Lewis, *The Four Loves* (New York: Harcourt Brace Jovanovich, 1961).

5. This illustration was used in a message by Bill Hybels of Willow Creek Community Church in Chicago, Illinois.

6. G. K. Chesterton, *Orthodoxy* (New York: Doubleday, 1959), 250.

CHAPTER TWO: THE STATE OF THE UNION

1. Robert Bianco, "The things we do for love," Newspaper Enterprise Association, © 1993.

2. Peter Kreeft, *Making Choices: Practical Wisdom for Everyday Moral Decisions* (Ann Arbor, Mich.: Servant Books, 1990).

3. Lewis Smedes, *Sex for Christians* (Grand Rapids: William B. Eerdmans Publishing Co., 1994), 111.

4. Walter Wangerin Jr., "Adultery Before It Starts: Clues to help you see it coming," *Marriage Partnership*, spring 1995.

5. Robert Wright, "Our cheating hearts," *Time*, 15 August 1994.

6. Wangerin, "Adultery Before It Starts."

7. Roberta Kells Dorr, *David and Bathsheba* (San Francisco: Harper & Row, 1986).

8. John White, *Eros Defiled: The Christian and Sexual Sin* (Downers Grove, Ill.: InterVarsity Press, 1977), 60.

9. Charles R. Swindoll, *Dropping Your Guard: The Value of Relationships* (Waco, Tex.: Word Books, 1983), 179.

CHAPTER THREE: A TABLE FOR TWO

1. Dr. James Dobson, "Men and Women: More Confused than Ever," adapted from *Straight Talk* (Dallas: Word, Inc., 1991), 2.

2. Smedes, *Sex for Christians*, 16.

3. Jimmy Evans, *Marriage on the Rock* (Tulsa, Okla.: Vincom, Inc., 1992). The genesis of the idea of types of destructive husbands and wives came from this book.

4. For a more detailed treatment of the needs of husbands and wives, see Ed Young, *Romancing the Home* (Nashville: Broadman & Holman Publishers, 1993).

5. Kevin Miller, "Are Men Bad Listeners?" *Marriage Partnership*, winter 1995.

6. Author, "Article title," *New Man*, January-February 1995.

7. Smedes, *Sex for Christians*, 163.

8. Clifford L. Penner and Joyce J. Penner, *Getting Your Sex Life Off to a Great Start* (Dallas: Word Publishing, 1994), 192.

9. Dr. Douglas E. Rosenau, *A Celebration of Sex* (Nashville: Thomas Nelson Publishers, 1994), 77.

10. Smedes, *Sex for Christians*, 208–9.

Chapter Four: A Table for Two

1. G. K. Chesterton, *The Common Man* (New York: Sheed & Ward, 1950), 141–3.

2. Evans, *Marriage on the Rock*.

3. Regina Barreca, *Perfect Husbands and Other Fairy Tales* (New York: Doubleday, 1993), 252.

4. Mike Mason, *The Mystery of Marriage* (Portland, Ore.: Multnomah Press, 1985), 81.

5. Archibald Hart, *The Sexual Man* (Dallas: Word Publishing, 1994), 106.

6. Rosenau, *A Celebration of Sex*, 187.

7. Mason, *The Mystery of Marriage*, 152.

8. Hart, *The Sexual Man*, 29.

9. Dave Barry, "Sex survey uncovers the thoughts of men," *Orlando Sentinel*, 1995.

10. Joseph Dillow, *Solomon on Sex* (Nashville: Thomas Nelson Publishers, 1989), 36.

11. Dr. Victoria Lee, *Soulful Sex* (Berkeley, Calif.: Conari Press, 1996), 78.

12. Smedes, *Sex for Christians*, 83.

13. Rosenau, *A Celebration of Sex*, 233.

14. Lee, *Soulful Sex*, 232.

Chapter Five: Pure Lovemaking

1. Oswald Chambers, *My Utmost for His Highest* (New York: Dodd, Mead & Company, 1935), 129.

2. Mason, *The Mystery of Marriage*, 126–7.

Chapter Six: "Where Did I Come From?"

1. *Newsweek*, 15 February 1993.

2. L. Kirkendell and R. Libby, "Sex Education in the Future," *Journal of Sex Education and Therapy* 11, no. 1: 64–7.

3. Barbara Defoe Whitehead, "The Failure of Sex Education," *Atlantic Monthly* (October 1994).

4. Stanton L. Jones and Brenna B. Jones, *How and When to Tell Your Children about Sex* (Colorado Springs, Colo.: NavPress, 1993), 119.

5. Ibid., 123.

CHAPTER SEVEN: "BUT WE LOVE EACH OTHER!"

1. Michael, Gagnon, Laumann, and Kolata, *Sex in America* (Boston: Little, Brown & Company, 1994), 102.

2. Karen Peterson, "Cohabitating first doesn't secure the knot," *USA Today*, 10 May 1995.

3. Philip Turner, "Sex and the Single Life," *First Things*, May 1993.

4. Peter Kreeft, *The Angel and the Ants* (Ann Arbor, Mich.: Servant Publications, 1994), 87.

5. Kreeft, *Making Choices*.

6. Mason, *The Mystery of Marriage*, 125.

7. Ken Rodriquez, "Driver's Legacy to Ex-lovers: Death," *Charlotte Observer*, 25 May 1996.

8. Ibid.

9. Ibid.

10. Tim Stafford, "Love, Sex and the Whole Person," *Campus Life*, December 1987.

CHAPTER EIGHT: JUST SAY YES!

1. Kim Painter, "Teens and Sex a Fact of American Life," *USA Today*.

2. Tim Stafford, *Sexual Chaos* (Downers Grove, Ill.: InterVarsity Press, 1993), 114.

3. Lorraine Goods, People On-line article, 1995.

4. William Shakespeare, "Sonnet CXVI," *The Unabridged Shakespeare* (Philadelphia: Running Press, 1989), 1302.

5. White, *Eros Defiled*, 148.

6. Joy Davidman, *Smoke on the Mountain* (Philadelphia: Westminster Press, 1954), 24.

CHAPTER NINE: GAY SEX

1. Stafford, *Sexual Chaos*, 133–4.

2. Dr. Jeffrey Satinover, *Homosexuality and the Politics of Truth* (Grand Rapids: Baker Books, 1996), 166.

3. Ibid., 51.

4. R. A. Kaslow, et al., "The Multicenter AIDS Cohort Study: Rationale, Organization and Selected Characteristics of the Participants," *American Journal of Epidemiology* 126, no. 2 (August 1987): 310–8.

5. A. P. Bell and M. S. Weinberg, *Homosexualities: A Study of Diversity among Men and Women* (New York: Simon & Schuster, 1978), 308–9.

6. Satinover, *Homosexuality and the Politics of Truth*, 21.

7. "Research Points toward a Gay Gene," *Wall Street Journal*, 16 July 1993.

8. William H. Masters and Virginia E. Johnson, *Homosexuality in Perspective* (New York: Bantam Books, 1979).

9. Irving Bieber, *Homosexuality: A Psychoanalytic Study* (New York: Basic Books, 1962).

10. Satinover, *Homosexuality and the Politics of Truth*, 227.

11. John Piper, *Future Grace* (Sisters, Ore.: Questar Publishers, Inc., 1995), 333–4.

CHAPTER TEN: SEXUAL CHAOS

1. Jill Laurinaitis, "A Lingering Horror," *Ladies Home Journal*, April 1995.

2. Lawrence K. Altman, "AIDS Is Now the Leading Killer of Americans from 25–44," *New York Times*, 31 January 1995.

3. Les Krantz, "Facts that Matter," Periodical, 13 March 1995.

4. Philip Elmer-Dewitt, "On a Screen Near You: Cyberporn, *Time*, 3 July 1995.

5. John Skow, "A Peeper's Paradise," *Time*, Date 1994.

6. Don Crossland, "Escape from the Trap of Addiction," *New Man*, February 1995.

7. Lewis, *Mere Christianity*, 91.

8. John White, *Eros Redeemed* (Downers Grove, Ill.: InterVarsity Press, 1993).

9. C. S. Lewis, *The Lion, the Witch and the Wardrobe* (New York: HarperCollins Publishers, 1994).

10. Ibid.

11. Gary Inrig, *Hearts of Iron, Feet of Clay* (Chicago: Moody Press, 1979), 248.

12. Ibid.

13. Satinover, *Homosexuality and the Politics of Truth*, 198.

14. Mark Laaser, *Faithful and True: Sexual Integrity in a Fallen World* (Grand Rapids: Zondervan Publishing House, 1996), 29.

15. Elmer-Dewitt, "Cyberporn."

16. Ibid.

17. Laaser, *Faithful and True*, 106.

18. Minirith-Meier Clinic, "Ask the Doctors," *Today's Family*, summer 1993.

19. Laaser, *Faithful and True*, 38.

20. Patrick Carnes, *Out of the Shadows* (Minneapolis: CompCare Publishers, 1983).

21. Piper, *Future Grace*, 336.

EPILOGUE

1. These "callers" are fictional composites inspired by listening to *The Single Connection* hosted by Ben Young on 26 May 1996. *The Single Connection* is a live, call-in radio program for single adults that is heard nationally. The topic on this particular night was sex and the single lifestyle.

2. Luke 15:11–32, *The Message*.

3. Henri Nouwen, *The Return of the Prodigal Son* (New York: Doubleday, 1992), 39.

4. Ibid., 85.